9783959058087
AF371555

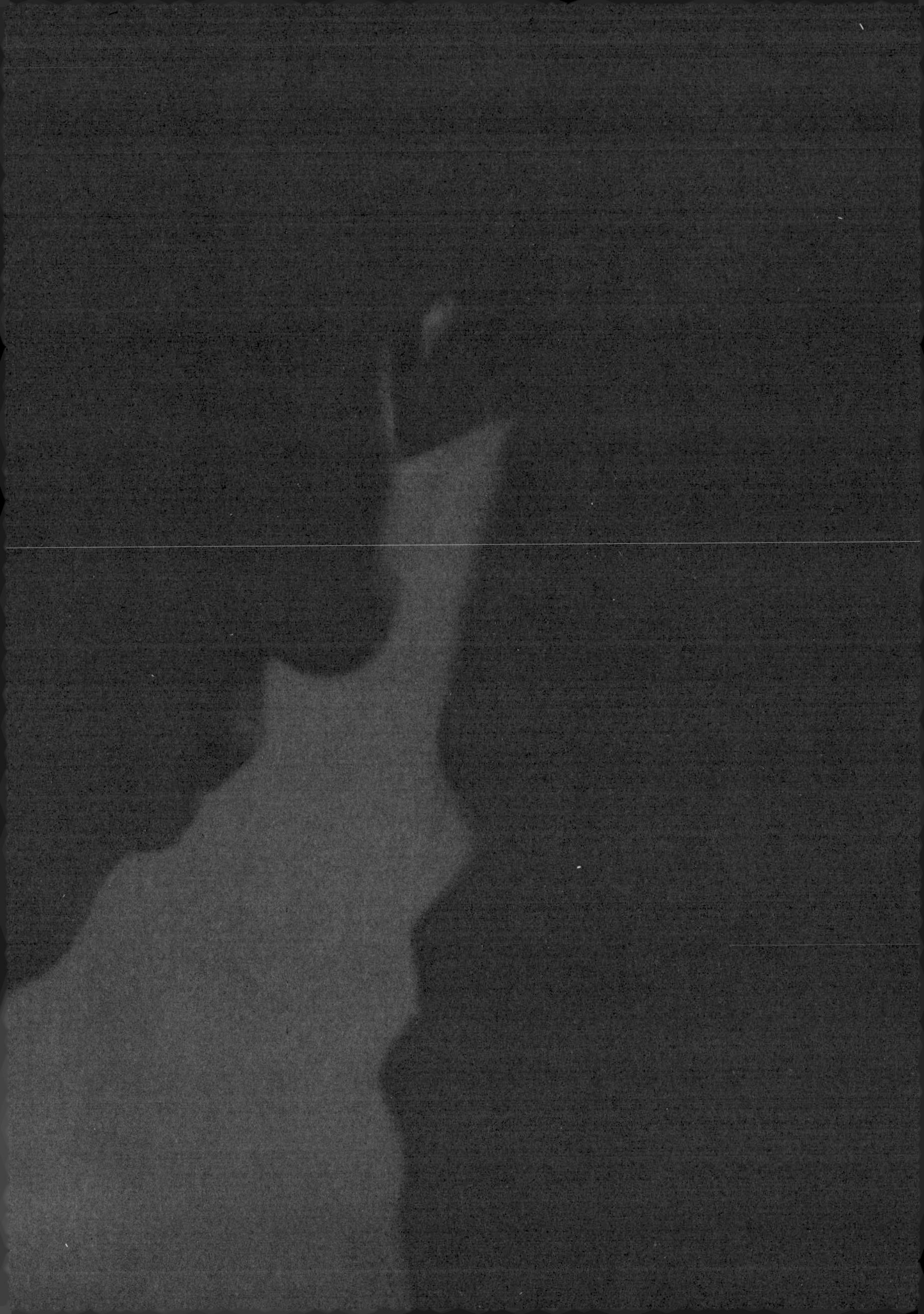

Pan Daijing

Haus der Kunst München
Tai Kwun Contemporary

Edited by Sarah Johanna Theurer

Spector Books

Introduction

This publication is born out of a shared mission and a collaboration between Haus der Kunst and Tai Kwun Contemporary. Both institutions strive to generate multifaceted, participatory and inspirational reflections on contemporary art with a focus on liveness and sound as fundamental practices of the present. Pan Daijing's work amplifies this impulse. Her live exhibitions are an invitation to encounter the self within the other or vice versa. They activate the public as well as the architecture of any given space. Brought to life in a world of increasing entanglement, Daijing's performances probe different modes of being in the world. Carried by immersive sonic landscapes that transcend conventional musical structures, the work metamorphoses into multiple formats and media, including music, performance, film, video and architectural intervention. The work defies all forms of organisation or categorisation and instead establishes a balance through exchange: You get what you give.

The book begins with a series of video stills, mainly shot during one of Daijing's frequent visits to Haus der Kunst. We see the artist at work, exploring the space through her body, through movement, tracing the building's scars. These contemplative moments are a prelude to her live exhibition *Mute* at Haus der Kunst in Munich (9.3.–14.4.2024). This book accompanies the exhibition and brings together a range of voices to interpret and pay witness to Daijing's work.

Resonating with its improvisational nature, the book is voluminous, soft and flexible. The text moves from the inside to the outside, reflecting the artist's wish to expand dimensions—of music, space, and time. Narrow borders emulate the quality of the fragile balance of coexisting opposites, of letters almost touching but never colliding.

Our thanks go to the authors, who are all in a close dialogue with the artist. To acknowledge this, we have included conversations between the artist and Andrea Lissoni, Artistic Director at Haus der Kunst; Xue Tan, Senior Curator at Tai Kwun Contemporary; and Emma Enderby, Chief Curator at Haus der Kunst. While the latter two evolve around specific works, looking back at *Echo, Moss and Spill* (2021–2022) and forward at *Mute* (2024), the former connects Pan Daijing's musical solo performances and her exhibition practice culminating in the opera *Tissues* (2017–2019).

In one of these conversations, Daijing notes that often, "the unspoken part is where the meaning lies." This is why the image sections form the basic structure of the book. From the beginning, Daijing adopted a critical stance towards the rapid circulation and consumption of images. It is rare to find footage of her live art. As an advocate of lived experience, she often creates situations that cannot be captured, recorded or represented.

The images in this book are chosen to reflect the artist's compositional intuition, not to faithfully document her performance work. Their focus is on development throughout time, without prioritising either one format or medium. In fact, many of the images are stills from videos, shot while moving with and amongst the artist and her performers.

The essays featured in this publication all relate to works that were created in the last decade, before and after Daijing had moved from Guiyang, China to Berlin, Germany.

Donatien Grau follows Daijing's paths across the histories of art, avoiding conventional ideas of heritage while embracing the sacred and the opera as conduits for unfiltered human emotion. Her work appears as an untimely bridge between the avant-garde movements and the current moment, reaffirming the im-portance of close and intense connections amidst a dynamic performance landscape.

Sarah Johanna Theuerer zooms in on Daijing's choreographic work in order to understand how the artist's use of landscape allows her to establish new connections between figure and background. Following the artist's passion for darkness and off-centre frames, she proposes a poetics of doom that is not at all pessimistic, but expresses how everything is both present and at the same time latently effective.

Both Raimundas Malašauskas and Lemohang Jeremiah Mosese approach Pan Daijing's work conceptually. Their contributions leave methodology aside, aiming instead to emulate the effects of Daijing's work. Mosese replicates the artist's episodic creations in a patchwork of thoughts on cinematic storytelling, masks, unpredictability and what he terms a "language of the in-between". Malašauskas mirrors her quest for liveness in a visual poem that recounts a work they had produced together. He touches on Daijing's relation to time and timing and describes her playing the space like an instrument.

Mark Harwood traces Daijing's enduring impact on an ever-evolving music scene. He analyses various compositions that traverse and intertwine the human voice and the machine, dissonance and harmony. He tunes into her sonic universe that transcends the essence of music or musicality. That "everything is music", as Daijing observes, is one of the many things we can learn from this book.

Edited by Sarah Johanna Theurer in close dialogue with the artist, the book is not an exercise in coherence. It gathers thoughts on what has shaped Pan Daijing's experience and practice. Therefore, and most of all, we would like to thank the artist Pan Daijing, whose work and unwavering commitment to complexity has made this book what it is: a sensual experience. Our gratitude goes to all those who have enthusiastically and generously shared their time as well as archival and photographic materials. We especially want to thank Sarah Johanna Theurer for the careful and considered editorial work, as well as to Florian Lamm for his thoughtful design, Jan Wenzel / Spector Books for the production and Daniel Ho, Senior Editor at Tai Kwun Contemporary, for his expert advice and steadfast support. We also thank Lydia Antoniou for editorial assistance and Jan Caspers for proofreading.

The extended period that Daijing spent in Hong Kong, from summer to winter of 2021, including a lengthy three weeks in quarantine confinement, was an important journey of arrival and process of new forms of language in the Asian context. Daijing's generosity of sharing and strong will to engage immediately shaped a community of artists, musicians and individuals around her. Her ambitious live exhibition *Echo, Moss and Spill* manifested her natural ability to lead collaboration. An openness for accumulation and experimentation made this body of work vibrant and responsive to the psychic space of Hong Kong in a transitional time, reverberating beyond the exhibition walls. We are grateful to the performers from Hong Kong, the entire team at Tai Kwun Contemporary, particularly the work of Senior Curator Xue Tan, Associate Curator Louiza Ho, and Curator-at-Large Tobias Berger, the work of filmmaker Dzhovani Gospodinov, as well as the support from our friends Du Yan and Li Lin.

Haus der Kunst extends a special thanks to Artistic Director Andrea Lissoni and Commercial Director Bianca Knall and their team, especially Biljana Gligorić. From the museum team we would like to acknowledge Curator Sarah Johanna Theurer and Curatorial Fellow Lydia Antoniou, as well as Chief Curator Emma Enderby for curating and producing the exhibition as well as the opening performances. They have been supported by the Haus der Kunst production team led by Hanna Kriegleder and assisted by Markus Brandenburg and Christian Leitner. We also wish to acknowledge the exceptional commitment to this project from our colleagues Claudia Illi, Janina Vujić, Peggy Rudolph and Anja Fetzer as well as Pia Linden and Thomas Kirst. We are grateful for the important input by Valerio Tricoli, Celeste Burlina, Kleber Nascimento, Charlotte Marr, the artist's studio and each of the performers who brought the work to life. In particular, we thank Chan Wai Lok for the privilege of his presence during the entire duration of the exhibition. Finally, and most importantly, we wish to acknowledge our sponsors and individuals whose support so vitally enables us in our ongoing commitment to shaping a transnational transformation in the arts.

Haus der Kunst München and
Tai Kwun Contemporary

Chronology

The following is a compendium of projects by Pan Daijing, who works as an artist, director, composer, musician, choreographer, performer and designer. Since her work constantly moves between and across genres and refuses easy categorisation this overview encompasses all formats and media. It prompts us to look at the complex commonalities between Daijing's various works. By no means exhaustive, it is an attempt to illuminate the cornerstones and key ingredients of important projects by an artist whose work may well end up defining a new genre.

Mute

Solo exhibition, survey with alterations of existing works and new commissions, spread out over 18 connected rooms, spaces animated by daily durational performance and activation performances, 8 performers

9.3.–14.4.2024
Haus der Kunst
München, Germany

Direction, music composition, choreography, spatial design	Pan Daijing
Cast	Chihiro Araki, Camilla Brogaard, Kelvin Kilonzo, Pan Daijing, Amie Jammeh, Leah Katz, Chan Wai Lok, Cary Shiu
Sound Engineer	Valerio Tricoli
Videography	Pan Daijing, Dzhovani Gospodinov, Kleber Nascimento
Architect	Celeste Burlina
Light design	Charlotte Marr
Commissioning institution	Haus der Kunst München
Curators	Sarah Johanna Theurer with Lydia Antoniou, Emma Enderby, Andrea Lissoni

P. 123

The Hour Between Dog and Wolf

Short film, 23:30 min, shot between 2021–2022 in Hong Kong

Direction, sound	Pan Daijing
Cast	Sylvie Cox, Pan Daijing, Christine He, Steph Lee, Chan Wai Lok, Pun Tak Shu, Leung Pak Ting
Camera	Pan Daijing, Dzhovani Gospodinov
Editing	Pan Daijing, Liyo Gong
Colourist	Dirk Meier

2023

P. 85

Until Due Time, Everything Is Else

Solo exhibition, 4 connected rooms, inkjet print, glass, 5-channel video, bone meal, volcano powder, sound, brushed metal, charcoal, gypsum board, plaster, water

23.9.–19.11.2023   Curator Tom Engels

Grazer Kunstverein, Austria

Dry Score

Charcoal on gypsum board with plaster and wall paint, 4 pieces, brushed metal displays

Grief Lessons

5-channel video, 2 projectors, 3 monitors, 3:22 min, loop

| Camera | Pan Daijing, Dzhovani Gospodinov | Editing | Leung Pak Ting Pan Daijing, Dzhovani Gospodinov, Liyi Gong |
| Performers | Sylvie Cox, Steph Lee, Chan Wai Lok, Pun Tak Shu, | Colourist | Dirk Meier |

Metal

2 fine art pigment inkjet prints glass, dimensions variable

Footnote

Bone meal, volcano powder, dimensions variable

Scale *Figures*

A pair of 8-channel sound pieces composed for 2 opera voices (installed across 2 different sites), a bridge connecting 2 warehouses, a pavilion overlooking an amphitheatre, stainless steel, white leather, silkprint, postcard, rubber

7.4.–9.7.2023 Gwangju Biennale Hall and Jungwoe Park, Gwangju, South Korea

Concept, music composition, technical direction	Pan Daijing
Product designer	Ximon Lee
Sound engineer	Roy Carroll
Commissioning institution	14th Gwangju Biennale
Curators	Sook-Kyung Lee with Sooyoung Leam

Avalanche

Short film, colour, sound, 3:30 min, shot at the Louvre in Paris

Direction, music	Pan Daijing
Cast	Sylvie Cox, Pan Daijing, Aya Sone
DOP	Stefan Ciupek
Editor	Dan Loghin
Colourist	Dirk Meier
Assistant director	Dzhovani Gospodinov
Costume design	Ximon Lee
Commissioning institution	Louvre Museum, Paris
Curator	Donatien Grau

One Hundred Nine Minus

Spiral staircase, single-channel loudspeaker, 2 opera voices treated with revox tape machine

1.5.–2.1.2022
Tai Kwun Contemporary, Hong Kong

Concept, music composition	Pan Daijing
Countertenor	Steve Katona
Mezzo-soprano	Marie Gailey
Revox treatment	Valerio Tricoli
Sound mastering	James Gainsbourg

P. 169

Echo, Moss and Spill

Solo exhibition, 3 flights of spiral stairs leading to 3 connected rooms, sound, 2-channel video installation, single channel live monitor, multiple loudspeakers, stainless steel, metal, cotton, red vinyl, ice, daily durational performance, 7 performers

16.12.2021–2.1.2022
Tai Kwun Contemporary, Hong Kong

Concept, direction, music composition, choreography	Pan Daijing
Cast	Sylvie Cox, Pan Daijing, Christine He, Steph Lee, Chan Wai Lok, Pun Tak Shu, Leung Pak Ting
Videography & co-editing:	Dzhovani Gospodinov
Opera singers	Anna Davidson, Marie Gailey, Steve Katona
Sound mixing	James Gainsbourg
Visual research	Richard Whittle, Zuzana Pabisova
Curators	Xue Tan and Raimundas Malašauskas, with Associate Curator Tom Engels and Assistant Curators Louiza Ho and Erin Li

Untitled

Intervention with a series of sound pieces taking over all rooms of the museum and its 3 story high entrance hall, haze, light, performative descent

27.8.2022
Mykolas Žilinskas Art Gallery, Kaunas with CAC, Vilnius

Concept, music, technical realisation
     Pan Daijing
Curator   Raimundas Malašauskas

Uncut

Flooding an abandoned shipyard on the bank of the Chao Phraya river, 13 large ice cubes, wooden steps, machinery, bandage, sound, light, loudspeakers, sandbags, 5 performers

29.10.2022
Bangkok Dock, Thailand

Concept, direction, music composition		Commissioning institution
Pan Daijing		Ghost 2565 Triennial, Thailand
Cast	Alin Charuamonchit, Paopoom Chiwarak, Pan Daijing, Janice Lau, Nitipat Pholchai	Curator Christina Li
Light design	Duck Unit	

Done Duet

600 kilos of steel, soaked in strong acid;
500 square metre space, half-filled with
white quartz sand; a pair of 28 metre high
silos, bathed in daylight; 2 opera voices,
17 metres of synthetic hair, acrylic plate,
steel anchor, single channel live monitor,
water dripping every 13 seconds, activated
by an opening performance

17.4.–25.7.2021
Power Station of Art, Shanghai

Concept, music composition, design, technical direction	
	Pan Daijing
Countertenor	Steve Katona
Mezzo-soprano	Marie Gailey
Visual research	Richard Whittle
Commissioning institution	
	13th Shanghai Biennale
Curators	Andrés Jaque with Filipa Ramos

Seal

Passage through a pitch black tunnel, empty Tresor Club, bandage wrapped around steel bars, haze, 2-channel video, opera voice, ice, lamp, precise entry and exit times

25.9.–30.10.2021
Kraftwerk, Berlin

Concept, music composition, technical direction	Pan Daijing
Videography, editing	Dzhovani Gospodinov
Countertenor	Steve Katona
Mezzo-soprano	Marie Gailey
Comissiong institution	Berlin Atonal

Half a Name

Series of site-specific mini-opera, presented by 3 performers, multiple cameras

Zeiss-Großplanetarium, Berlin
National Pantheon, Lisbon
Herrenhäuser Gärten, Hannover

Concept, direction, music composition
Pan Daijing
Countertenor   Steve Katona
Mezzo-soprano   Marie Gailey
Costume design Ximon Lee

2021

Half a Name Act I

2-channel video, colour, sound, 7:05 min

27.3.–20.6.2021
Surplus Space, Wuhan, China

Concept, direction, music
Pan Daijing
Videography, editing   Dzhovani Gospodinov
Curator   Mingjun Lu

Dead Time Blue

Atrium and the surrounding corridors of the galleries upstairs; empty galleries with glass doors filtering large HQI lights, stainless steel, black leather, soil, multiple loudspeakers, composition for 3 opera voices, 7 performers

30.1.–31.1.2020
Martin Gropius Bau, Berlin

Concept, music composition, choreography	Pan Daijing
Cast	Jia-Yu Corti, Pan Daijing, Anna Davidson, Marie Gailey, Steve Katona, Thibault Lac, Shade Therét
Costume design	Ximon Lee
Commissioning institution	Martin Gropius Bau, Berlin
Curators	Stephanie Rosenthal with Noémie Solomon

P. 63

Tissues

Solo exhibition, circular space, concrete walls animated by light and reflection in motion, multiple loudspeakers, black square carpet, wooden steps, foil, textile, 3 opera singers, 10 dancers, sound

2.10. / 4.10. / 5.10.2019
South Tanks, Tate Modern, London

Direction, music composition, spatial design	Pan Daijing
Cast	Gaby Agis, Richard Court, Jia-Yu Corti, Pan Daijing, Anna Davidson, Joseph Funnell, Marie Gailey, Steve Katona, Thibault Lac, Fernanda Muñoz-Newsome, Malik Nashad Sharpe, Rosalie Pearce Bell, Klara Utke Acs
Installation textiles	Ximon Lee
Wardrobe support	Samuel Guì Yang
Make-up design	Crystabel Riley
Lighting support	Marcel Weber
Videography	Dzhovani Gospodinov
Commissioning institution	Tate Modern, London
Curators	Andrea Lissoni with Carly Whitefield

The Absent Hour

Sound, light installation, loudspeakers, daily durational performance

2.10.–6.10.2019
South Tanks, Tate Modern, London

Music composition, choreography
 Pan Daijing
Cast Gaby Agis, Richard Court, Jia-Yu Corti, Pan Daijing, Anna Davidson, Joseph Funnell, Marie Gailey, Steve Katona, Thibault Lac, Malik Nashad Sharpe, Rosalie Pearce Bell, Klara Utke Acs

mm

Large rectangular sand island, outdoor swimming pool, surrounding corridor in the style of colonial architecture, skyline of a city, sound, multiple lights, 3 opera singers, 2 dancers, 5 performers

March 2018
Columbia Circle Shanghai

Concept, music composition, choreography Pan Daijing
Costume design Ximon Lee

P. 53

Tissues I:
A Prologue

Large glass pavilion with irregular shaped ceiling, tour bus, carpark, street lamp, surrounding streets, running tram, broken elevator, haze, textile,wind machine, white feather, light, 2 opera singers, 8 dancers

10.11.2018
Pavillon Sicli, Geneva

Direction, music composition, spatial design — Pan Daijing

Cast — Nabila Alegre, Tamara Alegre, Pan Daijing, Valentina Demicheli, Yinhan Deng, Mingqi Hu, Kayije Kagame, Kamilya Kuspanova, Julia Lind, Edgar-Allan Torres

Textile design — Ximon Lee

Wardrobe support — Samuel Guiyang

Make up — Franziska Presch

Curators — Andrea Bellini, Andrea Lissoni

Commissioning Institution — Biennale de L'Image en Mouvement, Geneva

In Service of a Song

Solo exhibition, video, colour, sound, 14:00 min, loop

17.2–17.3.2018
Eden Eden, Galerie Isabella Bortolozzi, Berlin
9–12.11.2017
Haus der Kulturen der Welt, Berlin

Performance installation, plywood, soil, sound insulating foam, gymnastic rings, acrylic glass, 1 tortoise; the solo exhibition included a 5-channel video installation of daily 13:00 min performance, loop

Concept, production, performance
    Pan Daijing
Commissioning institution for the performance installation
    Haus der Kulturen der Welt, Berlin
Curator   Martin Hossbach

Fist Piece

Stage performance, 3-channel video

Multiple locations worldwide, including Kraftwerk, Berlin; Elbphilharmonie, Hamburg; Barbican, London

Music, direction, dramaturgy	
	Pan Daijing
Performance cast	Pan Daijing, Gregori Homa, Yanwen Xiong
Film cast	Junying, Pan Daijing
Cinematography, editing	
	Ekaterina Reinbold

2012–ongoing

P. 141

Untitled Series

Solo stage performances, multiple locations worldwide

Recent works are supported by the artist studio team, among them Max Graef Lakin, Samatha Wolf, Qusay Awad, Taissa Fromme.

In Service of a Song

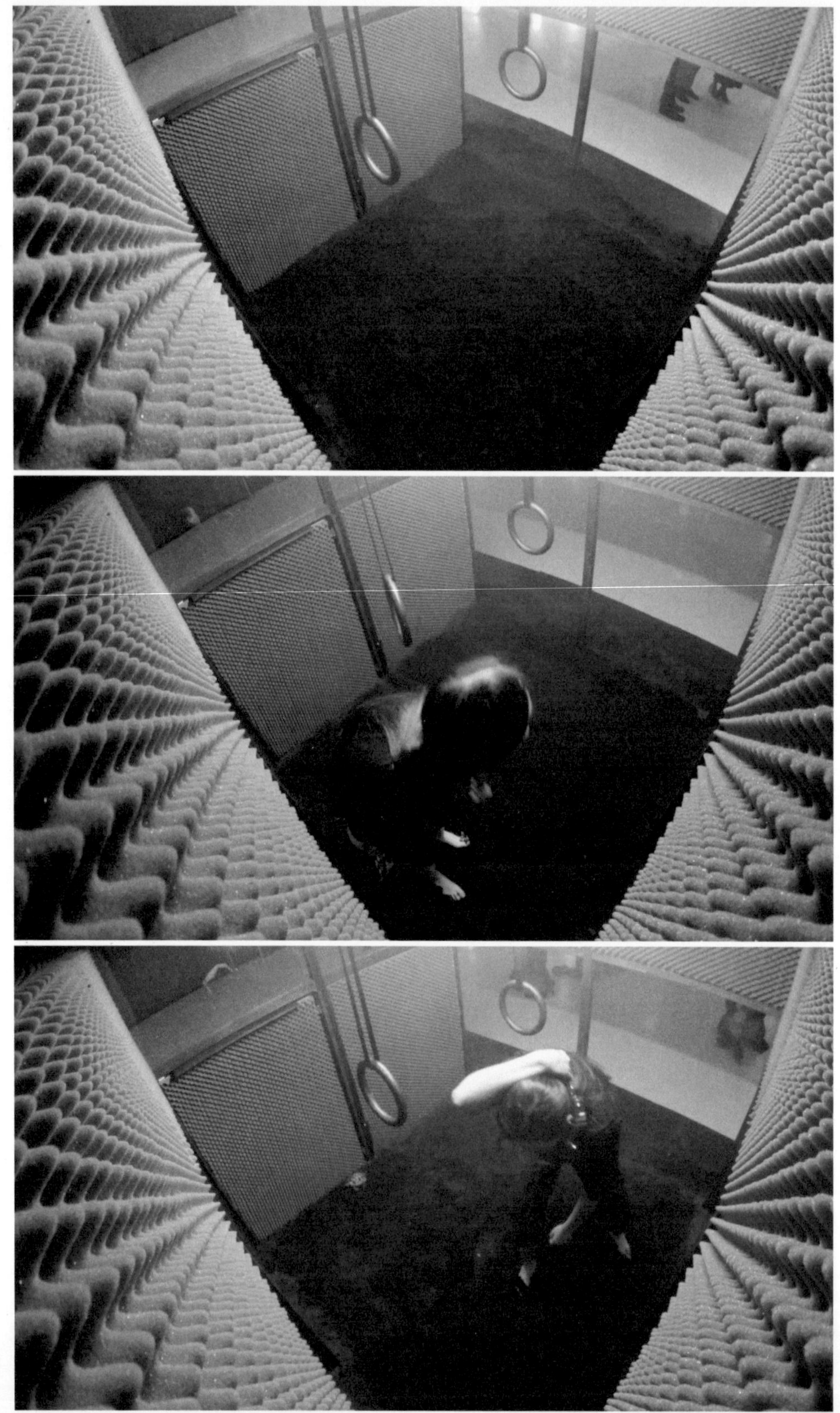

Raimundas Malašauskas
Unrendered

strictly
snoring
across
foam
and

(former)

glory

greek song
and sorrow
gulpable
hydrated
monstrous
detailz

a dizzy leap across
precarious balances
climbing from within
followed by the
meddley of middles

tales and toys

in sharp vocations
    a glitch reveals
        a secret
            of time
                whose shape
                    is a ghostly
                        stitch

                                as endless
                                    as finite
                                        as round
                                            as sparse
                                                as

                                                    in future
                                                        butterfly

                                                a drunk
                                                of
                                                inside a cave
                                            inside the track

                                    monsters
                                    snoring
                                    strictly
                                and
                            devoid of rational devotion

                                exit noir

                    from
                    we came
                    where
                    from
                    exit not far

                                EXIT

                                                of
                                                the sign
                                                as we approach

            shape

                    that change
                        from the past
                            former glories
                                unlinking

49

                                    and dusty
                                as audacious
                              as symmetrical
                             as effervescent

                                as trembling
strictly
      snoring

          sinuous locations
                building
                        insidious associations
                              spanning
                                    multiple chapters
                                         of never before
                                              and never after

          of nothing that you didn't know before, of nothing
          that you knew, of invocations and the trembling, of
          curvaceous slippages across, and drifty stitches,
          cringing, deliriously itchy, rampaging the air. Confi-
          dence comes in drops as in air, as in vapour, a thin
          veil of despair. Firstly, and lastly, time, an agonising
          artifice. "Believe me", it says, "believe me — I can
          burn slow"

       linking across centuries
              buoyant lights
                        arduous tremors, introspection in reverse
                              my life your life whose life
                                    forever life
                                         forever silent
                                              forever swagging
                                                  forever never life

                                         it spins
                                    in echoes, viscous echoes
                                grinding stretches
                              of smoke bereft
                         of anything that can still combust
                      encroached, expanded
                   dancing with a horizon
              long shelf-life

       suspended

          and the magnificent descent. In a spill of the sec-
          ond, she will be descending the stairs, stitching the
          Duchampian and the Medean realms seamlessly.

The bride, the crown, the golden fleece. The cephalopodian building of the gallery will keep sinking into her sound for another few minutes and reemerge several years later (as it was prescribed), when the renovation is over.

In 2022, I invited Pan Daijing to visit Mykolas Žilinskas Art Gallery in Kaunas, Lithuania. Closed for renovation a year earlier, the building of the gallery stood mute, suspended on the outskirts of time. From 1989 to 2020, it served as a hub for almost thirty years of programming of various manifestations of "plastic arts" (painting, sculpture, etchings...). This coincided with a relatively peaceful period in the history of Modern Europe. Conceived before the end of the Cold War and cast in a well-mannered style of postmodernism, the museum welcomed us as a "found building" — an obscure object, built from dolomite, glass, and steel, alienated from its mission, crumbling apart while the new roof is installed, cracks and leaks open to wind, rain, and dust, not to forget occasional music or dance festivals that would take place there. Our performanceinstallation might have fallen into the latter category, had it not been dedicated to the practices of grieving and listening to celestial and earthly bodies. It was called *Mars Returns*. The Roman god of war was explicitly brought back by the war in Ukraine that had erupted a few months earlier. Meanwhile, the planet of Mars was journeying across individual astrological charts of everyone involved — participants and visitors.

As Daijing stepped into the building, rain was running down the walls inside. We walked from room to room, from one floor to another, through one side of the almost symmetrical device — similar to a massive squid or a defunct robot — to another side of the same device, just on a different floor. We were unable to identify our positions clearly within that labyrinth. "What if you play this entire building as an instrument of listening?" I wondered. She disappeared behind an open door, and behind her words — they kept opening things up as she sampled the building with her senses. Four months later, she was back.

Daijing arrived with a carefully curated box of sounds, edited as a response to the visual and acoustic characteristics of the building. It was aimed at playing all those spaces and floors simultaneously. The box fit neatly in her pocket. It was an open composition of her sonic wonders — released and unreleased, but mostly — the ones that were transmitted in her exhibitions and music live sets. The gallery building incubated itself within that composition, hosting specific layers of the same track in different spaces, allowing people to wander inside a track while walking from one room to another. Music became the space in the most literal sense. I had never experienced it so vividly before — walking inside music, feeling the strokes of tone and frequency in my lungs, aligning with the debris of melody through my skin, as the melody was taking me to the next room. Two minutes later, something unexpected happened. She emerged from the dark mist on the top of the stairs and ran down. It was a magnificent descent — unscripted, light, and furtive, out of the box, nowhere to be found later. I still feel goosebumps on my skin. Those stairs will never be taking me to the same place again.

The next time we saw each other was at the edge of the world. We arrived from different sides of it (the edge), again following delirious slings of symmetries. I came from point three, she came from point eight, perhaps, like singing a song from the beginning and the end simultaneously and meeting in the middle. "Does life stop at the edge of the world?" I wondered about the liminal states of being between the various states of "live" that she spans. There is always a sense of limit and boundlessness there, within a single line that does not follow any timeline. It is a Milky Way under your skin

a tenderly violent discharge

                    in other words

                              if words prevail

       to no avail

               invocation and rendition

                  inscribed within a single cell

at the edge of the world
     is where I find myself many times
                          through those different doors

whose shape I draw with both hands simultaneously, like drawing a kiss with both hands simultaneously, the inside and outside of it at once,
twice, across the devices, across bodies, crawling
through doors and walls.

"One cannot be on both sides of the door at the
same time," I remember a philosophy professor
saying. In philosophy, it may be impossible indeed;
in sound and space, it may be a way to be: sound
and alive.

Tissues I:
A Prologue

Tissues

Deep Feelings

This text is an extended version of a public conversation between Pan Daijing and the Artistic Director of Haus der Kunst, Andrea Lissoni, which followed a listening or, as Lissoni put it, a feeling session of the opera *Tissues* (2019). The two revisit events and conversations that led to the production of this work at the Tate Modern in London and consider the human voice and contemporary forms of transmission.

Andrea Lissoni Tonight, I experienced again the reason why I think you're not a musician. You work with space and experience. What happens is so much more than listening. As I was lying here, I tried to remember what I felt the first time I saw you. This was at Sónar Music Festival in Barcelona in June 2017. I didn't see you, actually. But I remember you took over the entire room, even without any light show or the like. It was all coming just from your body. There were maybe 1500 people in the audience, it was very bright, and I didn't see you, but I felt something very intense. Not necessarily someone, but something. It's not about hearing "the voice of the artist" — it's about being in between their mind, their body, your body, and the space. And I wanted to open that space.

You remember, it wasn't easy to convince an institution like Tate Modern to give a solo show to an artist under 30, coming from China, with no artistic history, during the opening of Frieze Art Fair.

But it turned out to be a fundamental experience for the institution, for you, for everyone. I think every person who had the opportunity to experience *Tissues* in these five days will probably reconnect to that feeling they had in that moment every time they re-enter the space. Enabling the space to carry a memory and transform people through what they encounter, this is what I care about. It's not the institution generating the memory, but the people are creating the memory of the institution.

AL Well, the second time I saw you perform we were at London's St. John at Hackney Church, in October 2017. This time I was pretty close, on the side, you were wearing a dark red shiny leather coat and had your face covered in a semi see-through mask embellished with pearls and [due to a recent accident] you were using crutches. You were barely mobile, which added to the impression of a bodily intense performance. It was completely different to what I had experienced at Sónar. And then, in Winter 2018, I witnessed your work changing yet again: at Eden Eden, a project space in Berlin, you showed installations made of prior performance materials, they became something else. The exhibition was titled *In Service of a Song*. At first I recall echoes of Melvin Edwards, his sculptural work, its dialogue with raw and visceral music. I was intrigued by your constant transformation, and an

Pan Daijing The space you speak about is in our heads, too. The space that each of us owns. We often tend to block these spaces out for fear of what we might discover in ourselves. Music allows us to explore them. It doesn't matter if I am a musician or an artist — I work with the idea of musicality, and that can happen anywhere in space, in movement, and also in sound. Music is in our conversation right now, in us being here… Sometimes we're part of something that we are maybe not aware of and that's already music to me. But let's go back to the beginning. You have witnessed many of my solo music and stage performances that were almost like an exercise for the work I do now. What was your experience?

idea of "artwork" in which nothing stays fixed, but evolves and mutates across liveness, documentation, and transmission.

AL When I went to see you perform *Fist Piece* at the Barbican in London, I have to admit I was suspicious about this event promoted as a "visual and sonic spectacle", as I am generally suspicious about A / V performances. But you managed again to disrupt my expectation: instead of standing on the stage, you started from the Barbican's staircases and I think this was the first time I noticed your sensitivity to expand the space through your bodily presence and activity. The same happened shortly after at the London Contemporary Music Festival, where you presented a flute performance. I had invited some friends like the filmmakers Ben Rivers and Andrea Dojmi, imagining they'd have appreciated your cinematic approach to liveness, and you surprised me once again! You were playing the flute, moving around the space, and people were following you.

PD People often ask me, "What was it that caused the shift from music to art?" But to me, there was no shift. You have witnessed all these solo pieces, *Untitled Series*, where I started exploring the relationship of audience, performer and space and developed my improvisational methods.

You also mentioned my use of colours, the body, masks — these were all political instruments for me. They helped me not to become another's tool of speech. It was during these live solo performances that I exercised to conduct and orchestrate my own voice, in the moment, owning that room. I enabled myself to choreograph the audience, their relation to myself and the space. I experimented with confrontation, determination, or comfortable and uncomfortable intimacy. This happened mostly in the music context. Within the format of the concert, one has very limited means to transform the space. I couldn't take over a space for a longer period of time, pierce the wall, activate a corner, swing those doors open … what an artist is exploring is always framed and restricted by the context they are in. What was next?

Up until that time, I had known you as someone "playing electricity", as in noise electronic music. I didn't expect you to go acoustic. From there, we started seeing exhibitions together, and encountering unconventional art. You came to see and eventually meet Joan Jonas, her exhibitions, her performances. I really wanted to share with you how you'd belong to a family of artists that have unexpected, groundbreaking practices.

AL … but it had already been in your work.

AL I always felt there was something cinematic in your work that had nothing to do with screens, but with the way you organize space and time. I'm not at all a

PD It's not that I want to break expectations per se. I'm interested in the unknown, the uncertainty, and what it does to our minds. I never felt the need or urge to reproduce something because it had worked well in the past.

In *Fist Piece* at the Barbican, I was a single body amongst everyone. I remember I walked in with a mug of tea because I had lost my voice, and I had to take a lot of medicine to bring it back for that moment. I started with a stand-up comedy, talking, then singing, and, through this vulnerability, bringing everything as close to me as possible until I felt my single body merging with the room. This kind of experience still feeds into all of my work.

With the first iteration of the *Tissues* project in 2018, I had the chance to use a building as an instrument. And this instrument is also sounding the environment around it, the streets, the neighborhood. It took us six months to find the right architecture for the work, and we decided to take the audience there in a tour bus! … Your invitation enabled me to expand my storytelling into space.

PD I'm curious about how you understand the storytelling in my work throughout these different phases. Because you often talked about my cinematic approach, maybe because you were working at Tate's film department at the time and our later project *Tissues* at Tate was also in the framework of expanded cinema?

cinema specialist, but there is a tradition of artists' cinema that I am very familiar with. Think of Jack Smith, Tony Conrad or Liz Rhodes. But the film that was to me the key, that was so clearly part of the legacy of the *Tissues* opera, was the 1967 Wuxia film *Dragon Inn*. It also plays a major role in the later *Goodbye Dragon Inn* by my beloved Tsai Ming-liang. It completely changed my understanding of the nature of not only the artwork, but of the bodies within the artwork; they are no longer your own body and the bodies of the people in the space. Therefore, everything is expanded; layers of memories overlap and genders — filmic as well as identity ones — blend.

So, encountering your practice, I felt far more familiar with the tradition of expanding the boundaries between cinema and art than the one of music within art. It has been very difficult for artists like Meredith Monk, Alvin Lucier, or Alvin Curran to bridge that gap. The encounter with you was an encounter with someone from a new generation, from a totally different background, who was doing exactly this. I was impressed. Your practice is unique — but then again it's not unique, because it's "becoming", it's always becoming something else. This brings me back to when you guided me into your understanding of Wuxia cinema, the tradition of opera, and how this all resonated with you. Anyway, … where did it start for you?

PD I often think I still stand in the same place as on the very first day. I was about to leave San Francisco, this was around 2012, and it was the first time I performed my own music live. I had carried a bunch of analog synthesizers, a drum machine, and some other gear, which I had just gotten on Craigslist. I wasn't familiar with most of these instruments; I just played with them. It was a semi-illegal concert in a cave by the ocean. Because there was no infrastructure, people came with torches, and in the background, one could hear the waves coming, smashing against the small rocks. I can still picture myself in a blue worker's

AL Listening to music often triggers memories, even very precise moments. Recently, whilst listening to a piece by you, I had this strange experience: I couldn't connect what I heard to anything I experienced in the past. There were so many layers of voices, some seemed to come from a remote past, some were here with us. Yet others were in a zone in between. What is this iridescent universe of voices that we were exposed to?

AL The voice is uncanny because it's many voices. It's strange; I cannot decrypt it. It doesn't tell me anything but the togetherness of the world, it keeps you and everything in the state of fluctuation. And this is what I think is so stimulating to try to transport into the exhibition space. It's not about the moment of the miracle or the revelation. It's about the state of constant encounter and constant transformation.

overall, quite literally diving into the situation, and maybe 30 or 40 people standing in puddles of sand, torches in hand, listening. Hopefully, my journey will always feel like this.

PD It's so interesting to me that people would always look for protagonists, right? But sometimes, silhouettes carry more story. I am really intrigued by the fact that, when the moment is over, we can't recreate an experience. What happened to us stays unique to each of us. And that is, I think, the most romantic way for people to come together.

I consider the voices a distillation, like a perfume. It is a provocation or a trigger, something that holds possibilities but doesn't necessarily have a definition. The texture is composed of operatic vocalisation, sounds of metal, of synthesizers, but really, there's no definition of the source. It's the silhouettes that form a landscape in the space. I can sense the room is still wearing that space like a perfume.

PD I'm really glad you feel this way. When I write music, I'm trying to send a love letter to people who I don't know, that's why it's so strange. The piece we were hearing is composed of six works. They span eight years, beginning with *Tissues*, which actually goes back to 2015. Listening to the originals would probably take more than five hours.

And the constant transformation, or constant encounter, touches on my deep fascination with what we call human. All of our voices are very unique and it matures. It's our signature and at the same time we don't really have much control over it. The voice is something extremely vulnerable. We can manipulate and train our voice, which is why I'm so fascinated with opera voice techniques. The voice has a lot to do with how we connect to the world, this ever-looping tornado. It can momentarily feel hopeless when you give yourself in to the ups and downs. Psychology is a very Westernised typology, but I want to say I am more interested in treating sound in a psychological way rather than sonically or musically. I want to activate or penetrate the possibility of expanding one's inner space, pushing it to the moment in which one is willing to give in. And this feeling of letting go or not being able to let go is a very individual experience; it's a dialogue with oneself. I just open the door through music.

AL What you compose doesn't generate any form, but a constant flow. It's like entering a river and knowing the water is never the one that was running before. I'm drifting in it. How do you transpose this into space?

PD I have the deepest admiration for any experience of music, and I want to exhibit that in my work. Music is not just sound; it's so many things. When we are walking through a room, there are so many things that create the sense of music. I want to bring awareness to the potentiality of music.

I think most of the work we've done together really requires personal experience in space. Because you as the visitor are the collaborator of the experience. Your perception, your personal history, the mood, the smell, the outfit you wear on any given day, the restriction of your movement because your jeans are too tight… all this changes your experience of the work. Every detail matters. For example, if a performer comes close and touches your skin, what's the temperature of their fingertips? All of these details are musical, although it's not a music work per se. All these things need to be experienced in person. I shared in

AL What you describe perfectly encapsulates the in-betweenness of your work: If you were in the musical field, this would be called a medley (but it's not a medley). If you were in the traditional exhibition environment, it would have been a survey (but it's not a survey). And it also inspires the mission of Haus der Kunst: I don't believe in the legacy of modernity, grounded on the idea that I see something and read something in order to explain what it is that I'm looking at. But I deeply believe in forms of transmission based on bodily perception and in time. We have reason to hope this knowledge can become an opportunity to transform. And your assembly of voices will amplify this mission.

the beginning the idea of distilling a perfume of different pieces. I like this image, because you can never re-experience what has already happened, but you can interact with a corner of what that could have been. This is what I want to offer in my live exhibitions.

PD I think we should not forget trust, the trust to enter a space and to follow an invitation to approach it in a slightly different way. The person with the key, the space and the audience are all equally important in the sense that they all have a chance to experience something together.

Until Due Time, Everything Is Else

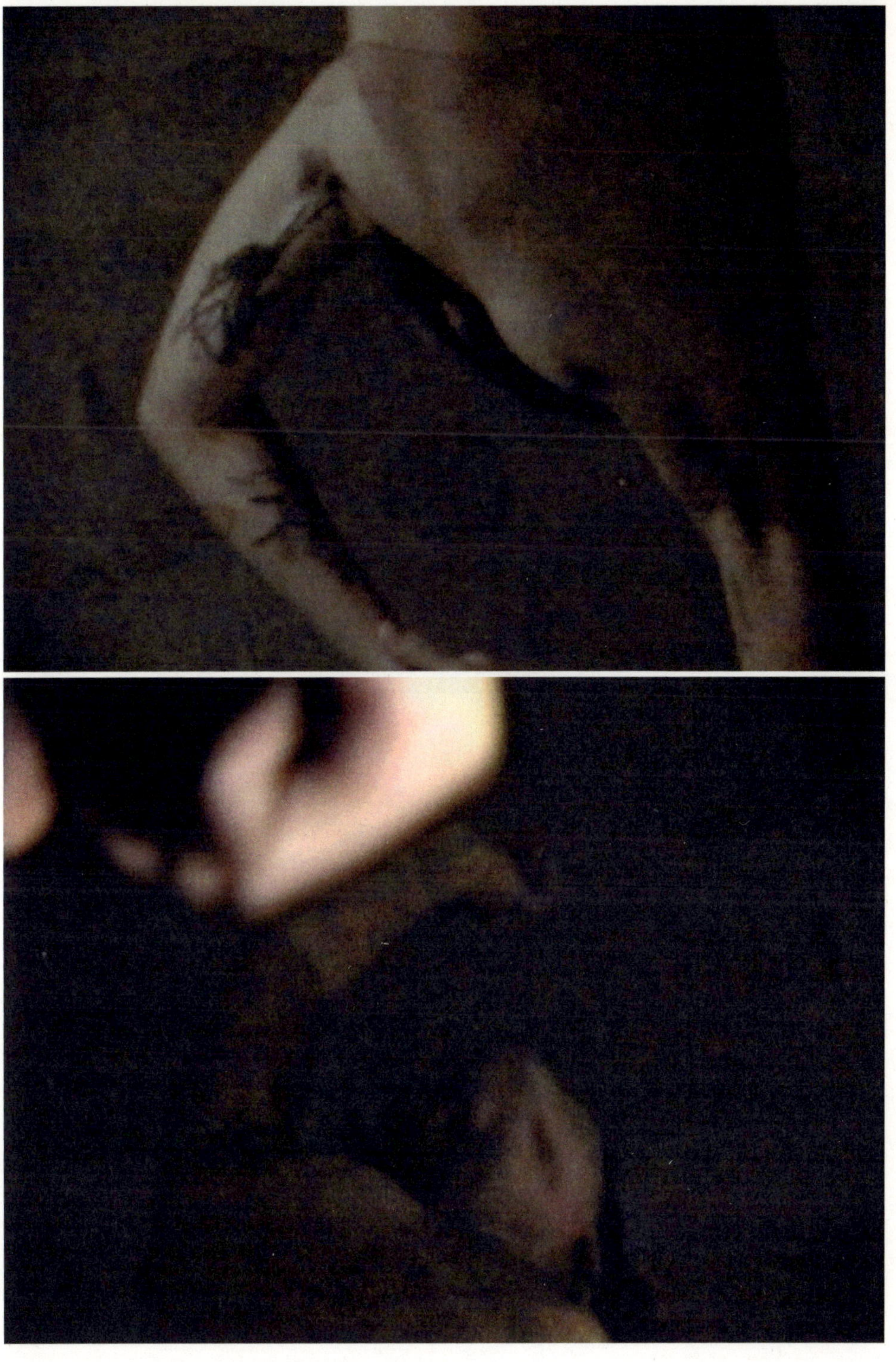

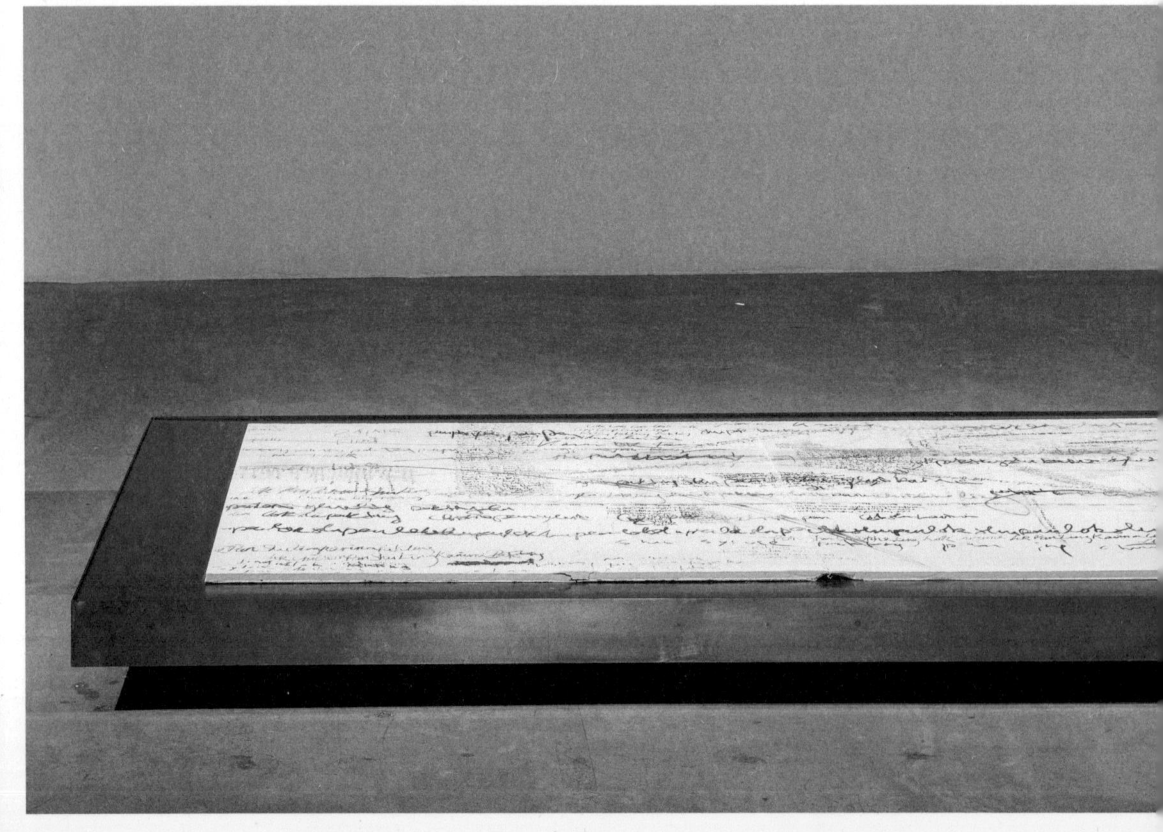

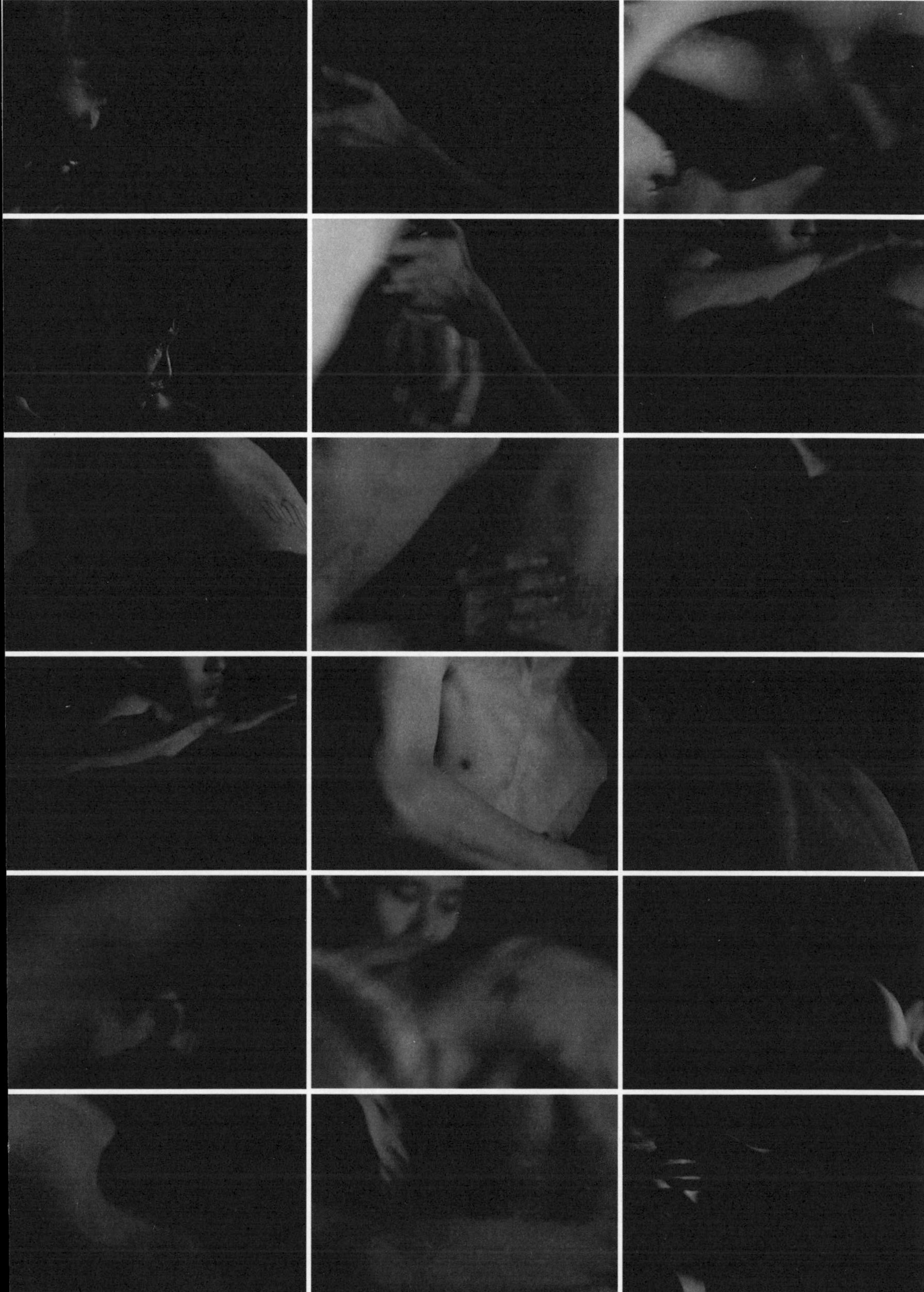

Donatien Grau
The Elegies of Pan Daijing

To be an elegiac means to miss. You do not really know what you miss, what was so important for you that you feel a violent grief that pains you and punctuates your heart. Was it the ideal? Was it love? Was it God? Was it family? What was it that mattered to you so much — and yet you did not know it made your life? You cannot identify it, but it punctures your heart. This is the description of the elegy. Pan Daijing's work is elegiac. To be an elegiac means to miss but also make the loss or the lack into a form of creation, into a melancholy that will never lose itself into nostalgia. It will increase life, not diminish it for the sake of returning to a gone world.

Pan Daijing's work can be characterized as an overflowing: of images, sound, sensations, emotions, life itself, at once laid bare and continuously moving and shaking. It flows from the life of the artist, from the score she establishes for her performances and films. It flows from her energy when she performs and goes to places so dark and bright no one would ever dare enter. It flows from her performers, fellowtravelers, who often reappear from one work to another. They are her company, through and with whom she feels comfortable going into the greatest discomfort. They, too, sense her impetus to be powerful enough to be more than life, for performing to be the fullest accomplishment ever offered to them so far. Pan Daijing's sovereignty is not a limitation of others, an attempt of imposing her own vision and erase theirs. It is the manifestation of evidence, of aura. It manifests in her own presence, her work invokes it at every instant: she creates aura out of almost nothing. There it is. Something is happening that is at once life itself and the sacred.

Witnessing her creative process, one cannot help but be struck by the sheer precision of it: the way this body part will interact with that one, the way this sound will break this other sound, and together, they will fight and become a lamentation, a cry, or an uproar. When Daijing directs, she decides everything: she may ask her performers to try out what they find interesting, but eventually, she decides, with pure authority. Her work is a creation from her dreams, from the worlds she was part of and left. She wants to return there and bring them out into the outside, for there should not be any separation between vision and actuality in the experimental space of art. In order to uphold such an exacting call for art, such a life-defining ambition, one needs no faint hearts for ambassadors. One cannot limit oneself or shy away from the greatest precision, for it will only enable the work to be what it was deemed to be.

The frightening ambition of making performance into the actualization of dreamscape and thus breaking the boundaries between mind and matter runs deep through Pan Daijing's heart and life. It is not a mere continuation of the "art and life" ambition of the 1960s, which aimed to defuse the separation between culture and the set by bringing the two closer than they had ever been, but rather the intensification of the stage at such a high level that nothing around can be left unharmed. Everything is so intense, so deep, it burns so wildly that it is difficult to return to the world afterwards as if nothing had happened.

In that regard, Pan Daijing's work could be described as anti-cathartic: it is not, according to a common reading of Aristotle's principle, the display of monstrosity as a tool to purify regular lives from such temptations. Her work is much more troubled and troubling: nothing is clear, the city may not be reunited at the end — the very purpose of tragedy — but we will have lived intensely in it and thereby remain in the memory of art. She lays it out all open for us to sense where life is and where it does not go, where angels fear to tread, and where they fly happily. Her work is intense, but it does not emit any judgment, nor does it convey any didactic message. Quite the opposite: she refrains from making any statement, any assertion. She does not say nor hide, she signals. Therein lies her greatest power — not assertion but manifestation.

As a matter of fact, her work in its entirety could come across as a system of signals: not one sound, one affirmation, but multiple, consistently contradicting signals that voice "I am alive. We are alive. And there is no contradiction." The individual and the structure around it do not have to be antagonistic, but can in fact interact and expand ways to be in the world: this is a rather obvious statement, and yet Daijing's work highlights it, not with a limited, light approach, but with extreme density. It is true of her vision and of the action of each performer, of the audience, of each work, and of her entire oeuvre. For it is already clear that one work leads to another, dwells on another, builds up on it, plays with it, and that this constant redefinition is the space she inhabits.

These dynamics equally apply to the patterns of art that preexisted her: she goes to places yet untouched but also pierces through the vein of history and time. Considering her work from the point of view of tradition may seem far-fetched, for she so clearly aims for radical pieces that redefine their very setting. However, her embrace of opera as a form is far from meaningless: in opera, language is very much present, but, being tied to sound, it is a straightforward manifestation of passion and emotions. Sound and words are brought together and yet, eventually, emotions overrule every preparation, however elaborate it may be. It is then understandable that Daijing would have chosen this genre: instead of conceiving sound pieces as such, of separating them from the continuity of history, she has decided to embrace opera, not as a closed-off road, but as a direct way into humanness. Opera is not simply the past, it carries elements of the sacred. Pan Daijing does not let herself be limited by preconceived ideas on heritage and the contemporary — "opera is so passé" — but creates her own paths across art. Usual characteristics do not apply to her: the fact that opera would come from the past is neither positive nor negative, ancestrality is not an asset or a problem. The only thing that matters to her is the energy of life and the fact that opera — in this case — is a direct take on it. She is entirely dedicated to the completion of forms while offering herself fully to the flow of art — both at the same time. The one thing to which she does not lend herself is a constellation of references. What she does is art, not culture: it does not follow any rule but its own and humankind's.

The gift of bodies to a greater cause manifests itself through long duration and physical intensity, pain even. One needs to strive, make efforts, and be ready, only because we know it matters. What could be considered gratuitous, dangerous, irrelevant by some, is profound and transformative to believers in art — such as Pan Daijing. Her community is one of people who believe that it makes sense to give everything to art, that it is not madness but the real form of sanity. The choreography of bodies is not dance as a form, it is the outburst of the soul. Sound is not a meaningless utterance, it is the song of the soul. Through every sound she brings into her works, she lets the soul — hers, the collective's — voice itself, directly, without mediation or message. She contradicts the pace of the instant, and opens it up to criticality. Being present does not signify giving everything to the fleetingness of the moment: it means taking in all the times, and having them present in oneself all at once, which will allow for the greatest sensation of the action. This sense of presence is tied to her great romanticism and mysticism in art: what may come across as deconstruction or even destruction is in fact an expression, one that does not require an explanation, and that just is. Sounds and movements together express something of the soul, of the way humans live, that is profound, intimate, and collective. In literature, writers have told their own story, at times with the most glaring details, for they considered the most intimate to be the most collective, something that everyone could relate to because it was exposed. Her art does not allow for anecdotes, because it stems from sound and bodies. It goes straight to the essential, even if it encompasses hundreds, or rather thousands, of sonic and physical decisions. There is no narrativity, not attempt at telling you a tale. There is a story, but it is not there to be told. The fact that it is there is what holds everything together. However, a little like a signal, there is no need to know it: one can merely let oneself go into sheer experience. If suggesting is the dream, Daijing has made intensity into a form of suggestion in its own right: a space where one is not hammered with a message, but induced to feel, imagine, let sensations take over from our rational minds and bring us to places dark and light whose existence we never agreed to recognize. She explores the most profound places of herself, of the performers, and of all of us. Every tension of sound and bodies is part of such an exploration, as is every release. She invites us to consider life, not from the point of references, anecdotes, artificiality, but to return to its very source, to be reborn at the fountain of existence, whose flow keeps pouring and pouring.

It can appear a little difficult to define precisely the framework in which to reflect on Pan Daijing's work, for it is such an event, in the proper sense of the word: something that "happens" and thus changes the course of how we think about things and look at them. The comparison to the rise of performance in the 1960s may appear misleading — "art and life" — but it nonetheless provides food for thought to decipher Daijing's work. The 1960s, in Europe and the United States, two parts of the world where the artist decided to live, the one after the other, were a moment of late modernity. It was not yet the imperial rise of postmodernism, and the sense of the "grand ennui", as George Steiner called it. Modernity needed more, it needed to move. Abstract paintings were not enough. Demiurgic sculptures did not deliver anymore. Performance was an answer to the quest for presence and meaning. It brought together subcultures, archaism, futuristic tones, creating a heterotopia, a space where things that would have never been deemed possible in society happened, where times collided and life was at last laid bare to be perceived. Thus it was cathartic. What was once the mandate of theatre became that of performance art. Bertolt Brecht no more, Artaud was the rage.

This may be one of Pan Daijing's genealogies. The decisive participation in the lineage of opera, the blurring of temporalities, the call for presence, the radical inscription within the heterotopic nature of performance: all of those traits of her work converse with such a genealogy. As Nietzsche famously said, the untimely is the most contemporary way of being. Daijing pushes this dynamic even further: the 1960s were a time of assertion, of different ways to make art and to live. She does not belong to that moment in history, she does not need to break from global culture in candid ways. There is no way to break away, trying will fail, no matter what. The solution is to force the experience upon us, something so powerful and melancholic at once that we will have to live differently. Power and melancholy are by no means contradic-tory ways of feeling: proving to all of us that they can be combined is Pan Daijing's greatest contribution. It is the very thread of her work.

My heart laid bare could be a Pan Daijing title, if she phrased what she does not want people to know. Every work is her heart laid bare: not in a metaphorical sense, but literally. Every time we witness a performance, we see blood coming in through the arteries, coming out, we hear her heart beat, once, twice, at times almost imperceptibly, at other times so strongly it frightens us, it beats, not drums, a heart. Attending a performance of Pan Daijing's is like holding her heart in one's hands — having that responsibility. The level of intimacy at which she performs is unfathomable.

Behind every work is life, her life, and ours too, for she gives herself so much she can nail the depth of her existence to it. Performance, since it started, has been the modern way to make the interaction between the individual and the collective into an emblem. It assumed that this connection, which had become increasingly tenuous, could be a space for experimentation, designed to say something about us humans. The birth of performance art at the beginning of the 20th century — as a field separated from theatre and music — responded to an archaisation of these older formats, to the rise of collective cultures, whether pop or political, and aimed at opening up a space that could be the mise en abyme of humanity.

Today, collective cultures, pop and political, are the order of the day and archaic at the same time. Daijing proposes an answer, which is to return to the roots of timelessness and presence, in a space that is not limited to either perception, without disconnecting timelessness from presence, or establishing presence as a refusal of everything else. Fulfilling both opens up a new, radical space, where art can reinvigorate itself and the world around it.

The philosopher Tristan Garcia described intensity as a "modern obsession", the horizon of a life that will require meaning and energy to survive across a then meaningless world. "There is no God, everything is possible," as the famous phrase goes. Intensity was one response to the rise of meaninglessness. Pan Daijing is intense, and so is her work. She has embraced intensity as a form of life, uncompromisingly. She will give everything to fuel the fire of art, she will lose herself, regain herself, let performance be the moment of self-loss for the sake of something higher, purer, for the instant of peace she reaches when it is about to end — the very last minutes of the performance, as it is about to finish, it is not over yet, and we are already on the other side. In these minutes, her face, which is often visible, has this peaceful, meditative expression, she is in ecstasy.

Pan Daijing's work could come across as modern: her belief in art, her commitment to it, the fact that she gave everything in her life to be who she wanted to be, to do what she wanted to do, lead us to take for granted that she is a modern artist. As she explores secret parts of life, her dedication to intensity and depth, also converses with those who then made the choice to live in and with art. But did they have a choice, or was it their mission, their calling, their mandate, to give themselves so that life could be laid bare and thus expanded? This modern question is Pan Daijing's. Her acceptance of and dedication to intensity accounts for a modern life. And yet, this modern life seems outmoded today: it is a romantic and fluid bridge between the individual and the collective, not the rhizomatic loneliness of the present. At a time when we historicise the modern era, considering it to be part of the past, Daijing proves that it is still relevant — by

and with her own example. She is fighting to prove that intensity can be right, that connections can be deep and fluid, and that this does not need to manifest itself in the refusal of the past. The past is not a set of references, it is a river, in whose flow one may get lost: the river of time and life, in which one never bathes twice, and which, however, continues to flow, always changing, always remaining itself.

Describing art as modern does not mean it belongs to the past, nor does it mean that it has to be part of an ideological, political construction: that is, the theorising that went on after the very artists that made modernity created their work, and determined the champions for its canon. Theorising has frozen modernity, some artists still burn and prove that the impetus to be in direct connection with time and the present is not dead. Pan Daijing ranks amongst those. Everything that is part of modern art as life is hers, including the thought, the consideration, the meditation, the shyness, the assertion, the authority, the incredible evidence that everything she does is what it should be, even when it is a mere, vague attempt — you have no idea what it will be, but she already knows, she knew from the beginning without putting words to it.

Modernity may come across to some as a future-driven, positivist attempt at governing the world. For many artists, it was a way forward amidst the helplessness of their present. However assertive Pan Daijing's work may be, formally, in its construction, it is always a melancholic outcry. And thus, it constitutes an elegy. It is a long song, telling us of lost worlds, of sadness, of darkness, of melancholy, of all the places we went through without knowing while artist knew, of the life-defining longings we were not ready to take in while the artist was, of the hopes for a more intense life that would have its own meaning which we were too safe to consider while the artist did. Every fragment of her art is a radical answer to the Hölderlin question "why poets in times of distress?".

Avalanche

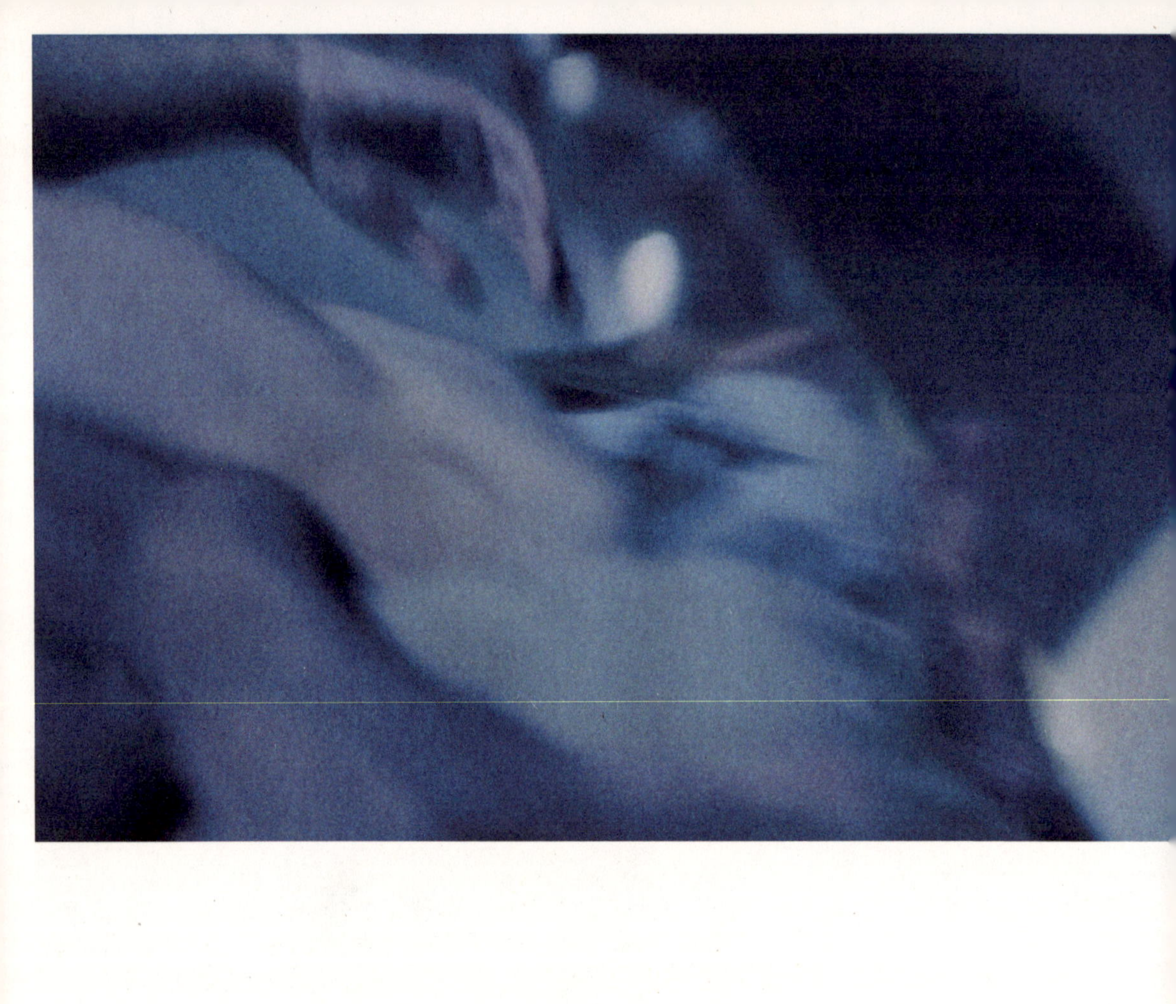

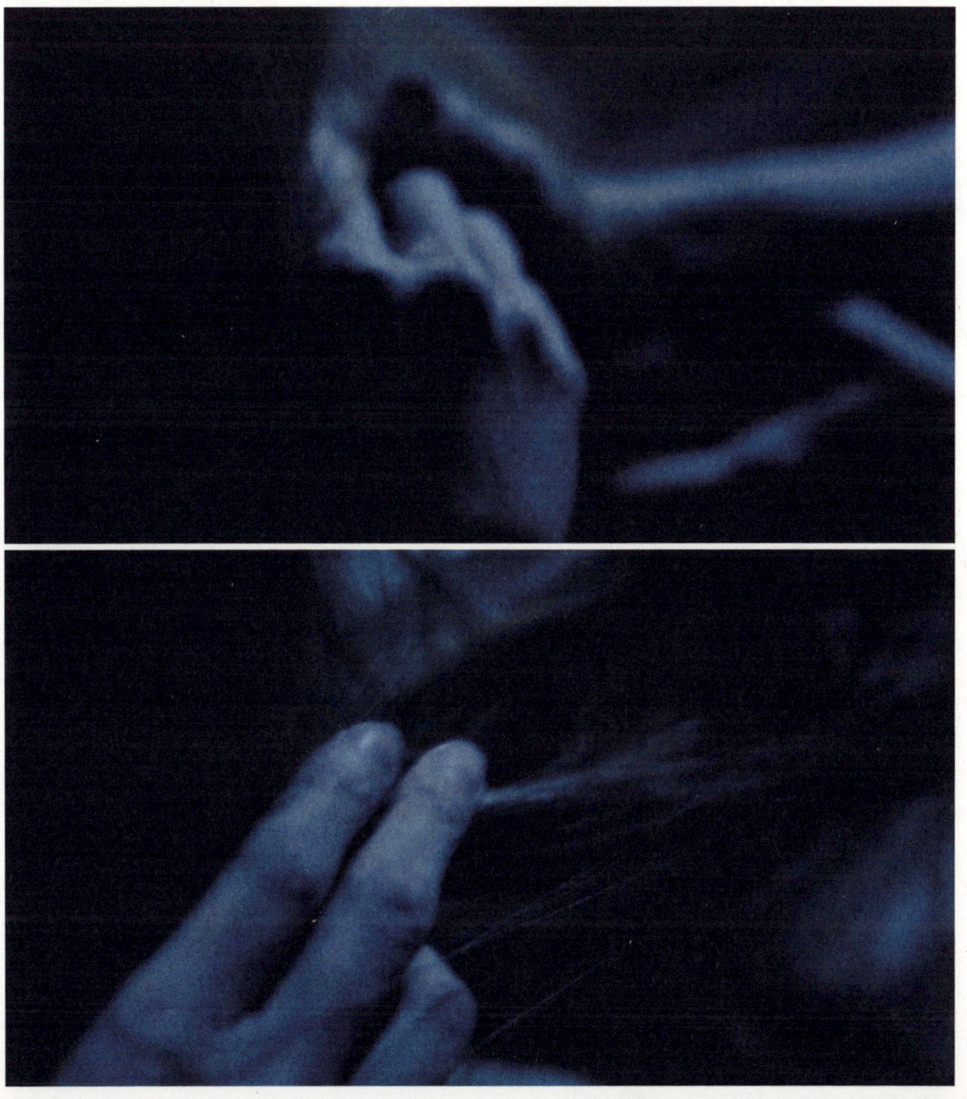

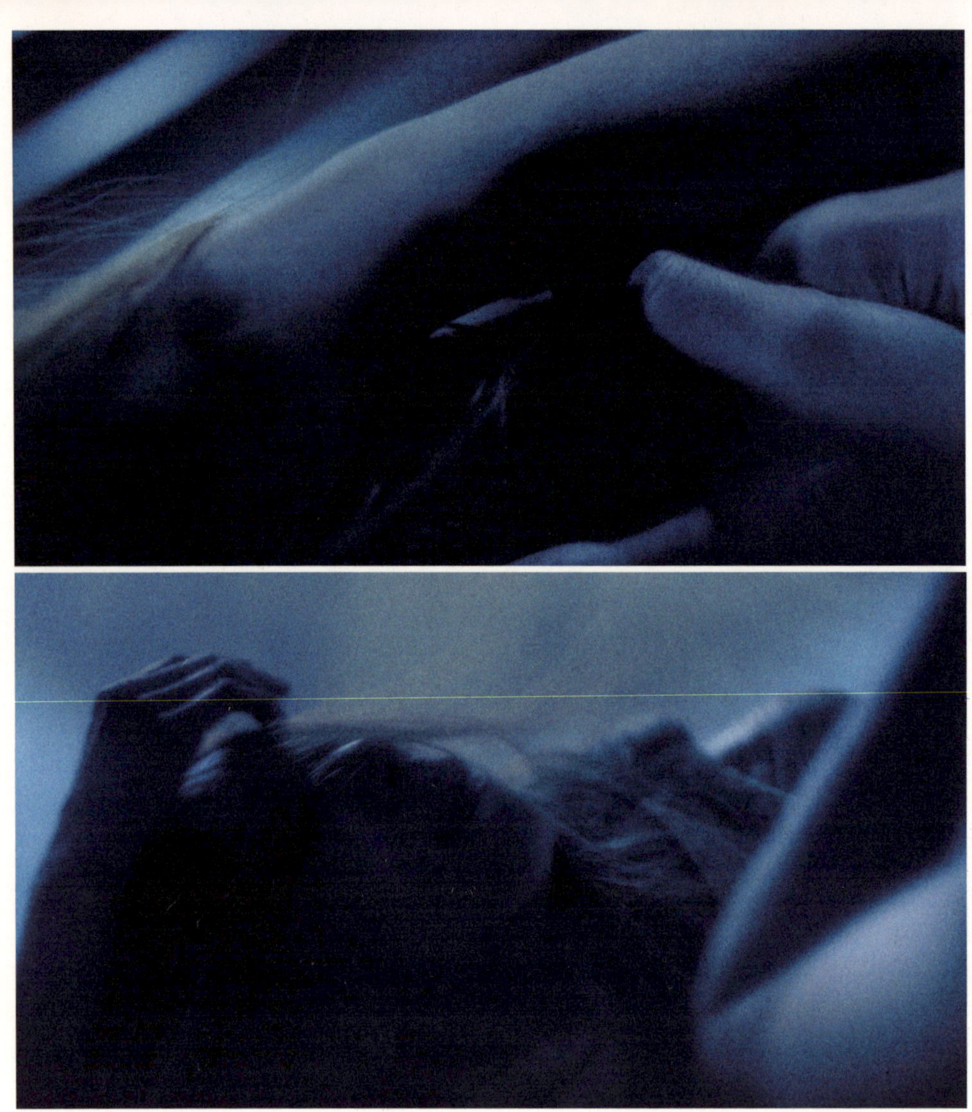

Lemohang Jeremiah Mosese
A Visual Odyssey

Written by fellow artist and filmmaker Lemohang Jeremiah Mosese, this text is an artistic response to Pan Daijing's work. It sheds light on their shared interests. To Mosese, dissecting an artist's methodology seems akin to unravelling a secret that even the artist themselves need not fully comprehend; he, in turn, opts for opacity.

Pan Daijing's visual odyssey joins poetic, visceral practice and evocative imagery in an intricate dance between allure and disquiet. Her artworks act as profound provocations, instigating an unsettling yet compelling atmosphere that prompts viewers to interrogate societal conventions and reevaluate their own perceptions.

In the imaginative realm of thought, I perceive Daijing as a compelling orator who has sewed the soles of her feet upon the landscape of her face. She carries a burning zeal to share the nuances of her encounters with the world. Daijing's tales are not just stories but sensory experiences–the taste of the soil touched by her feet, the essence of the air tasted by her tongue, and the profound silence that her ears embraced. Her narrative unfolds against the backdrop of a childhood spent in solitary reflection, a period marked by isolation and loneliness.

In contrast to the bustling urban environment, Pan Daijing's attention was drawn to the often-overlooked minutiae of life — the subtle nuances of smell, texture, and other elements that weave an intricate tapestry, forming the very fabric of her being. She emerges as a walking collection of emotions, a testament to her coming of age. In the quiet moments of her past, she forged a deep connection with the world around her, assembling the impressions of her surroundings onto the canvas of her soul.

Despite the solitude she endured, Daijing harbours an intense desire to communicate. This yearning extends beyond mere conversations; it transcends the boundaries of her own experiences. At times, she assumes the role of a deity in diapers — a childlike figure that finds comfort, unafraid to play with her own urine, to taste it and to make the audience taste it. She dares to test boundaries and pushes against the constraints of societal norms. In her fearless experimentation, she discovers that the perceived discomfort is not as daunting as it may have seemed.

In this two-fold exploration, Daijing navigates the realms of fascination and disdain. Within her work, one cannot help but sense the lingering essence of an abandoned soul. Her fascination with the surrounding world overshadows her interest in fellow humans. Filtered through her lens, humanity takes on a monstrous and sometimes almost hateful quality. It is a portrayal shaped by the deliberate use of distortions, purposeful movements, and the creation of a dark ambience accentuated by concealing the face with a mask. The deliberate use of these artistic elements transforms the familiar into something disconcerting. Daijing crafts a unique perspective on the darker facets of the human experience.

In moments when she approaches a member of her audience and locks eyes with them, her gaze evokes a subtle unease. The willful act of instilling a sense of discomfort within the audience is an integral part of her artistic expression. This sensation of unease serves as a canvas, allowing her to embody a creator's complex akin to a deity. It compels the audience to grapple with the unconventional facets of the human experience that lurk beneath the surface.

Pan Daijing strikes me as someone who actively seeks to engage and acknowledge an audience. It's as if her zeal is not just for communication but for a profound engagement that breathes life into others. She rises above mere interaction and animates the core of those who encounter her, much like sculpting living tableaus reminiscent of the mountains that once adorned the landscapes of her childhood. Her intention is not merely to showcase the dreamy and enchanting aspects of her world but to invite the audience on a journey into the depth of their own humanity.

Paradoxically, there also exists an undeniable beauty within the human performances orchestrated by Pan Daijing. The touch, the merging of bodies in a unified chorus, and the formation of a collective entity transcend the darkness. It is a celebration of the grace found in human connection and expression. Daijing's intentional eye contact with the audience or fellow performers adds a further layer of intimacy to the performances. These moments are like silent proclamations: "I see you, and you are beautiful." The darkness and distortion become a canvas on which the individual paints an alternate reality, one that acknowledges both the monstrous and the beautiful within the human experience.

In Daijing's works, bodies come to life, resembling a patchwork of flesh. It is as though they are being intricately and deliberately joined together. Occasionally, a process assumes the character of a deliberate act of severance rather than a harmonious convergence. This represents a calculated deconstruction of preconceived notions and established paradigms, an intentional dismantling that is a requisite precursor to the act of reconstruction.

Pan Daijing's artistic expression reveals a captivating paradox: as if enticed by siren song, the audience willingly steps into the immersive experience Daijing has meticulously devised. Yet, within this enchanting embrace lies an undercurrent of rejection. The contradiction establishes a captivating duality, a perpetual cycle where invitation and rejection coexist in harmonious tension. The act of inviting the audience into her world becomes a form of rejection in itself as they grapple with the discomfort embedded in every gaze exchanged and every emotion shared.

In her quest to forge an intimate connection, she constructs a maze of contradictions, where the audience is simultaneously drawn in and pushed away. The vicious circle, defined by its continuous oscillation between invitation and rejection, becomes a mirror reflecting the complex dance of human emotions and relationships. In this intricate dance between sewing and severing, creation and dissolution, Daijing undertakes the task of unravelling the tapestry of familiarity, a courageous endeavour that transcends the mere act of building. This deliberate deconstruction is not an act of wanton destruction but rather a methodical unveiling. It is a ceremonial shedding of the old to pave the way for the emergence of the new.

As the artist navigates this liminal space, a sense of surrender pervades — a surrender to the unknown, a relinquishing of the familiar moorings that once tethered the mind to the shores of certainty. It is within this profound moment of surrender that thoughts grow eyes and wings. The absence of anchors, once perceived as disorienting, metamorphoses into a liberating force, propelling the mind beyond the confines of the quotidian.

Thus, within the crucible of deconstruction, she discovers or stumbles upon the alchemy of creation — a process wherein the dismantling of the known becomes the catalyst for the birthing of the unknown. And yet, this may appear as an artist's sleight of hand, a deft trick to an uninitiated observer, when in reality, it is a subtle ruse to court the embrace of slumber. It is not an artifice of the creative mind but a stratagem designed to traverse the ethereal domains of dreams, where the mind can grow eyes and wings.

Pan Daijing and I often find ourselves immersed in twilight dialogues, exploring the chasms between the known and unknown, the underground and the surface, the paradox of residing in between. We are conversing in the language of the in-between, and find commonality in fusing the vile and the sacred. Her approach epitomises conflict, traversing the boundary between light and shadow, beauty and the macabre, the handshake and the fist. I see touch as a common thread: a sensation experienced through skin, cloth, wall, or stone, at times gentle or turbulent, yet unceasingly graceful.

One striking aspect of Daijing's work that resonates with me deeply is the constant quest for a place. Perhaps it's because we both inhabit a space between two worlds: the countries of our birth and our migrant lives in Europe. For years, I harboured the conviction that I would eventually return to Lesotho. And yet it took me over a decade to acknowledge that the imagined place of return no longer exists; it resides solely in the utopian realms of my mind, a beautiful yet essential deception that sustained my endurance in Europe.

Pan Daijing's creations evoke a sense of home, of an unrestricted sanctuary, an imagined place that need not manifest physically but can be inhabited in the ethereal dimension. Her artistic voyage is an immersive experience, a journey marked by intensity and unpredictability, blurring the demarcation between artist and audience. With an audacious display of vulnerability, she defies the norms of live artistry, inviting spectators to confront their emotions and embark on a profound exploration of the intricacies of the human psyche.

An extraordinary facet of Daijing's work lies in her unapologetic defiance of conventional morality and contempt for established norms, unmistakably evident in her unconventional artistic approach. Her visual works serve as a breach in normative aesthetics, drawing audiences into an eerie and disquieting sphere.

I think one must recognise that the contradictions embedded within an artistic expression are not merely endpoints but rather a transformative journey — a rite of passage towards becoming that resonates with the legacy of Jamaican writer and cultural theorist Sylvia Wynter, whose ideas revolve around the reconceptualization of human beings through the transformative process of passage. The contradictions within Daijing's creations serve as catalysts for metamorphosis. In navigating the discomfort and unease that is woven into the fabric of her art, viewers undergo a transformative journey reminiscent of a rite of passage.

It is through the tension of contradictions that the audience is invited to confront, deconstruct, and ultimately reconstruct their perceptions.

The Hour Between Dog and Wolf

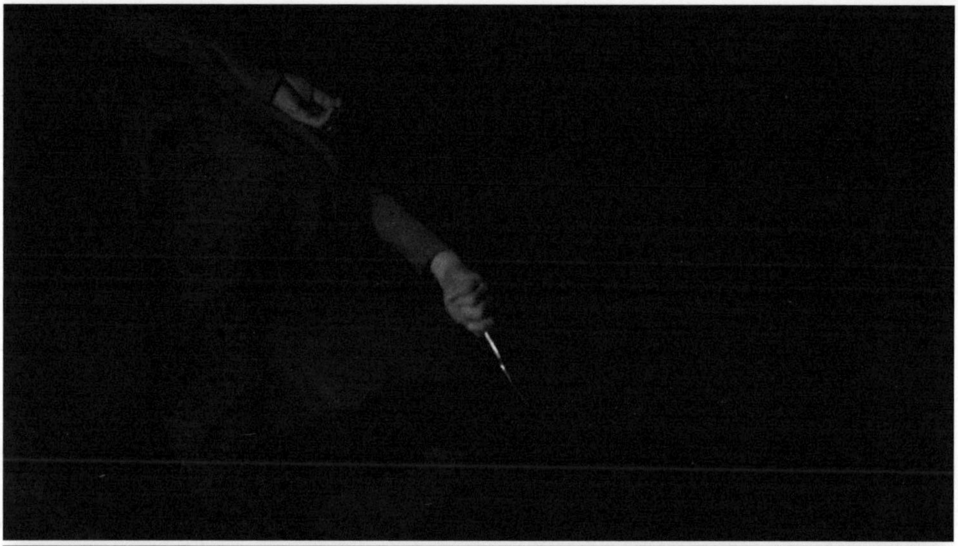

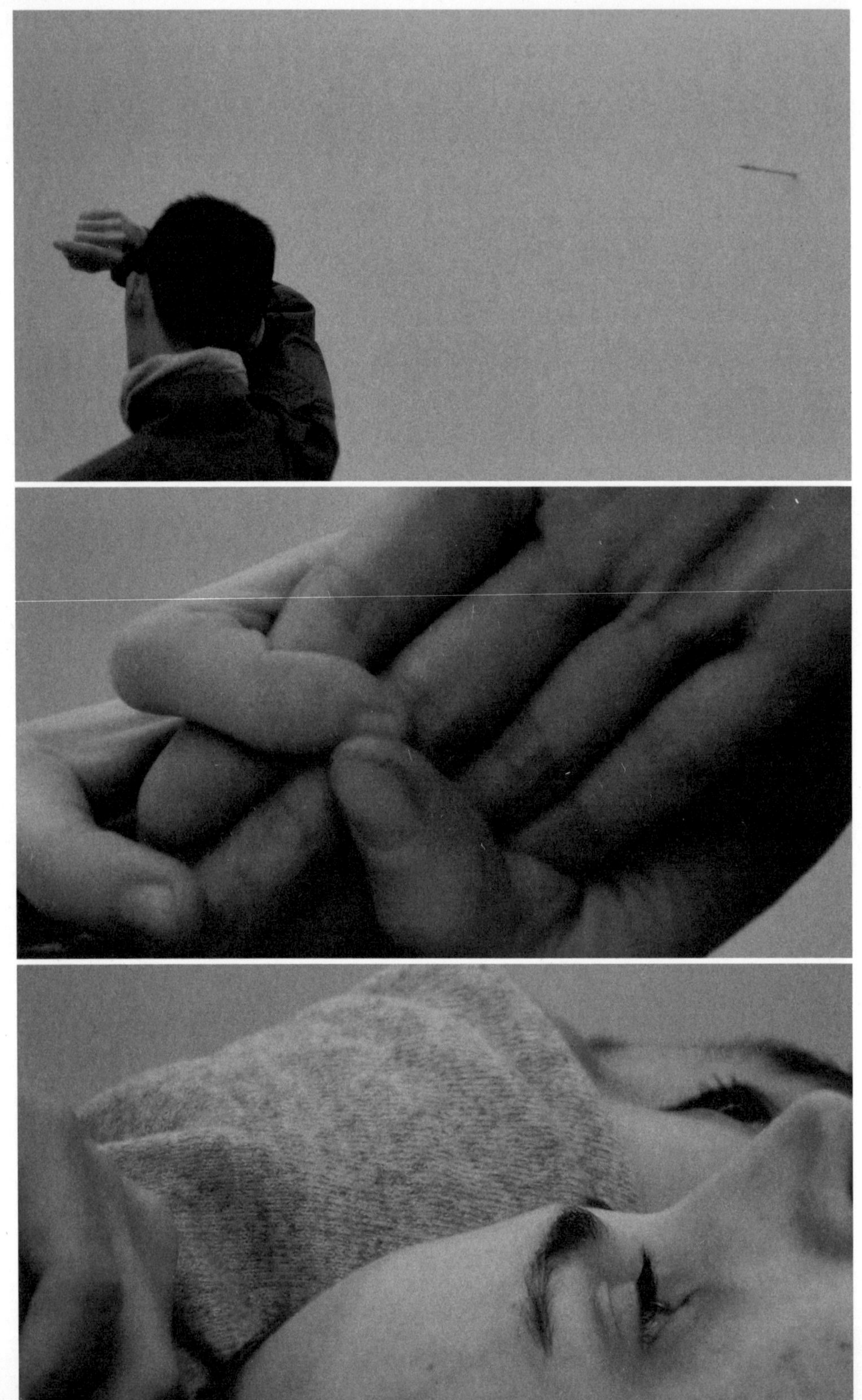

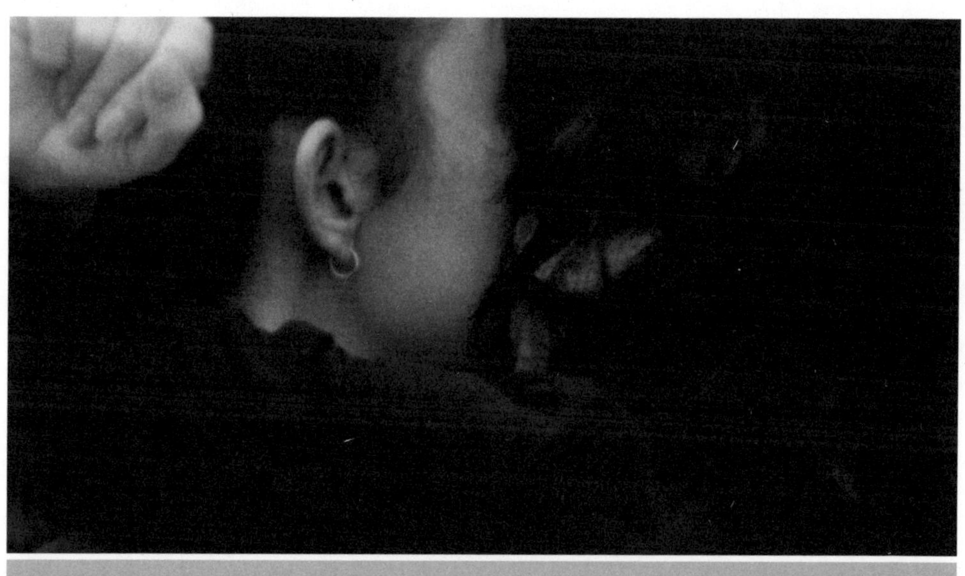

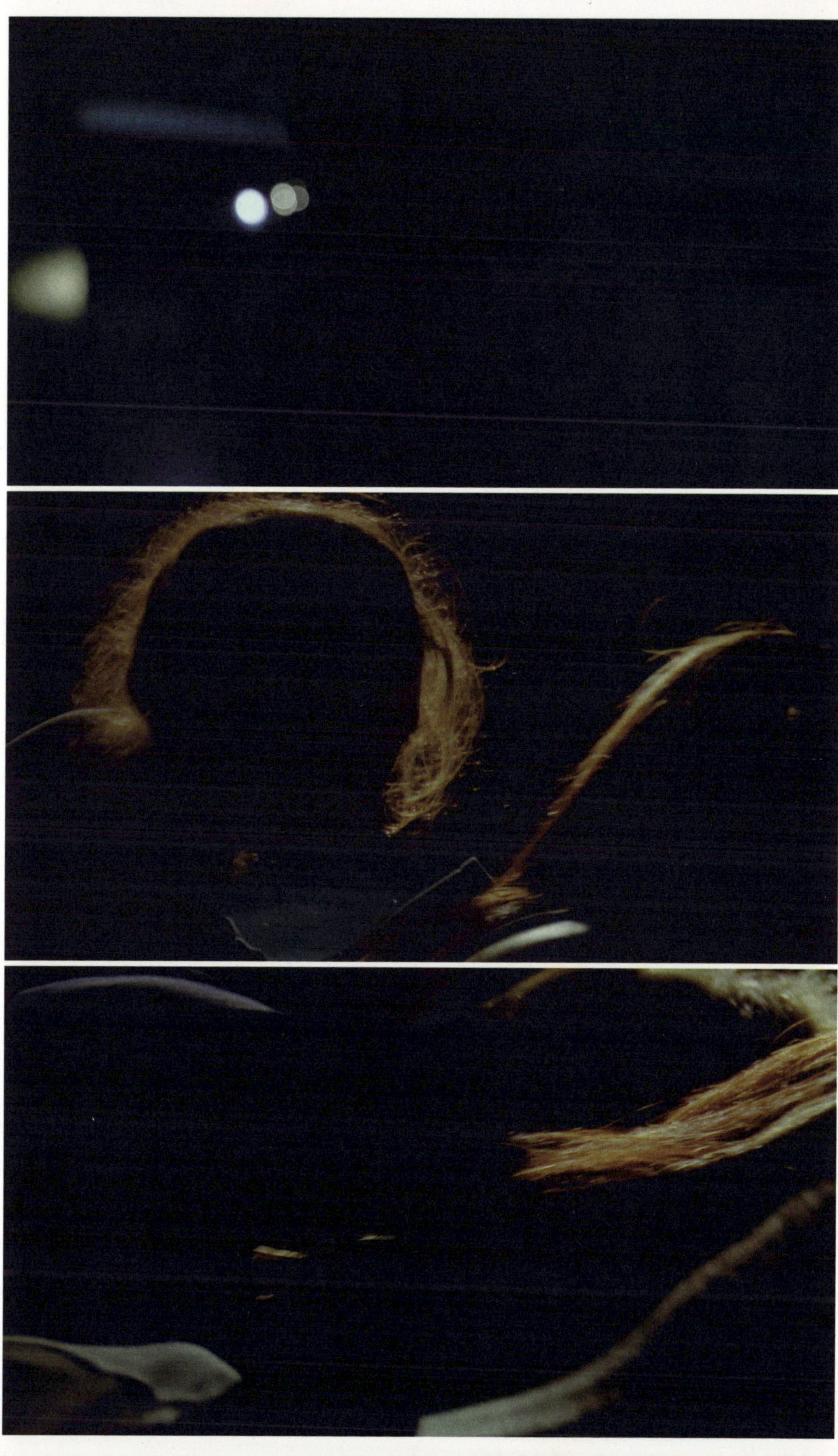

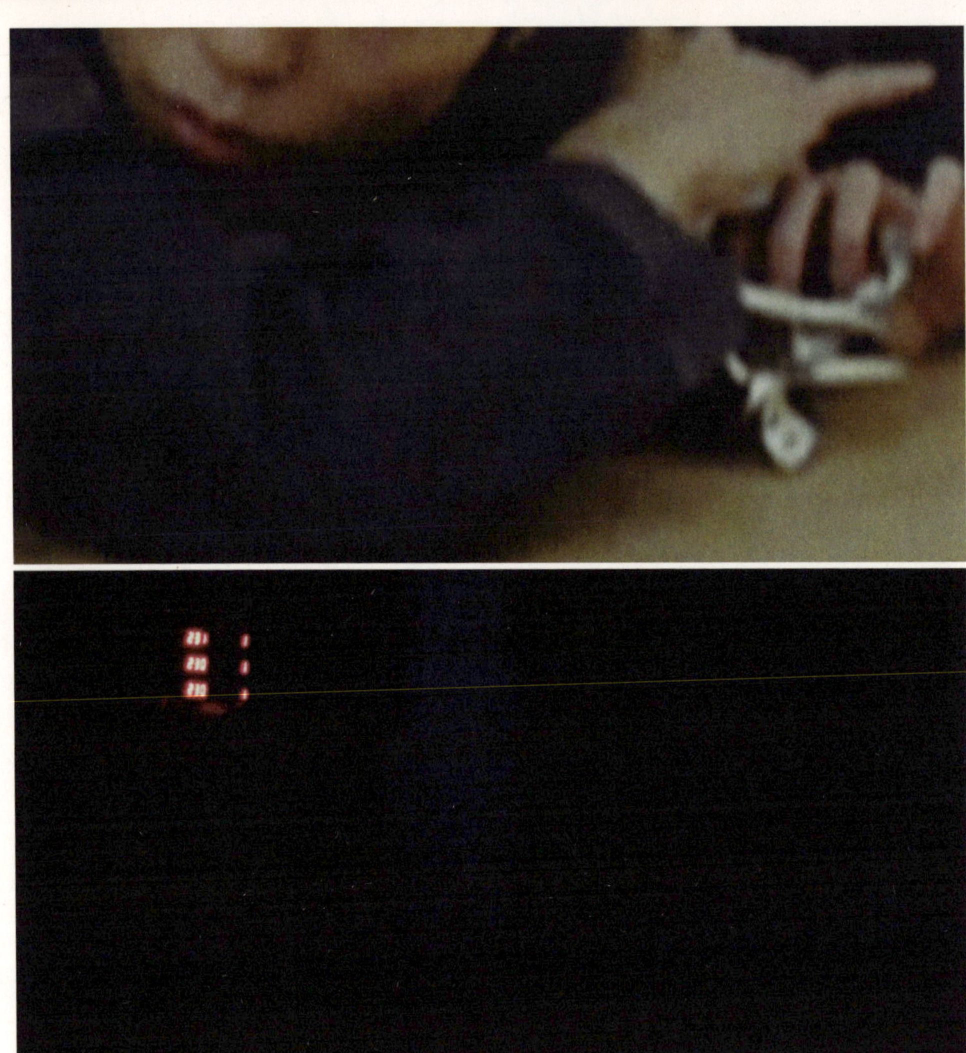

Mark Harwood
With a Vocal Cord Yet

"These talking machines are going to ruin the artistic development of music in this country. When I was a boy… in front of every house in the summer evenings, you would find young people together singing the songs of the day or old songs. Today you hear these infernal machines going night and day. We will not have a vocal cord left. The vocal cord will be eliminated by a process of evolution, as was the tail of man when he came from the ape."
— John Phillip Sousa, in *Arguments Before the Committee on Patents of the House of Representatives*, 1906

"I feel like I'm muted unless I'm making music"
— Pan Daijing, borshch magazine, 2021

Sousa was correct; the advent of technology allowing the recording of music transformed the music itself and the means by which it was distributed and engaged with. Young people singing songs to each other in a local community is undoubtedly an exquisite experience for all, but it does have its limitations regarding the dispersion of information.

In time we lost neither the human voice, nor the soul. Rather, the voice has continued to exist and evolve in and amongst a wide variety of mediums, whilst the soul has consistently found new ways of expression. An endless advent of new audio tools and means of reproduction has appeared since the birth of audio reproduction. Alas, it has not killed the voice nor the soul. The ghost within and what comes out of the machine is our friend if we let it be.

All material is instantly transformed by the act of preservation. Human activity captured via the means of recording opened up an infinite opportunity to play with the matter of the recording itself.

Pan Daijing's musical output is a stridently contemporary version of human expression via the tools at hand today, not by any means hiding in the machine itself but allowing it to open up that which lies inside her. Daijing has often mentioned that her approach to making an album is not to enter the project in order to make a grand statement, or even an album as such. Everything in her labyrinthine output constitutes an amorphous expression of the human self.

In this extraordinary age of hysterical media saturation, ultra-accelerationism, and a thick fog of fake, loud, threats, both real and not, there is an intense but calm inquiry in her work. Hers is an art free from temporal tropes that incorporates all manner of the historical pedigree. Her mind, as a tool, executes the breath of being. Daijing has built a peculiar form of music around a variety of elements: recent and ancient history, new pain, old thoughts, sound as voice, and music as tradition, simultaneously torn apart. Paradoxically, this is a kind of music that eschews traditional roles of music as it transforms into a pure expression of form, from within.

Her music takes shape in many forms: recordings, live performances, operas and spontaneous situations. The voice serves as a pivot point in many of these presentations. Given that Daijing's live performances are based on so much improvisation, there is an enormous amount of musical matter that appears on a particular occasion and will never be heard again. Pan Daijing is not an artist who makes albums and then tours those albums, playing tracks from the latest release for the purpose of promotion. Like the music in a performance, an album is simply a snapshot of a greater whole.

In 2015, a tape in an edition of 50 copies was released by the German label Noisekölln. Each copy featured handwriting by the artist. The tape is called *Sex & Disease* and consequently gives a unique statement of intent in the form of a harrowing and intense take on contemporary electronic music. This is not an "early phase" developmental work but rather a heavy and demanding framework for future explorations created by an artist with an immediate sense of purpose. *Sex & Disease* is an instrumental precursor to the subsequent prominent vocal explorations.

Like the body of work that branched from this debut release, *Sex & Disease* is a sincere study of the power of sound and the power of expression that derives from the simplest of gestures, the pressing of a record button. The ability to record allows us to document, and the ability to document provides a canvas that can be painted in thought through this medium we call music. Pan Daijing knows this very well, and as a result, this initial release brims with the inside being externalised through sounds, suggestions, atmosphere, and mood. The track *Sex* was recorded in one take on a single instrument. The sounds and suggestive turns of the knobs on the tools present a harrowing take on the act of repetition inherent in the act of the title. It continues from there. You know how it goes. Here, it is presented with irony and truth. The truth outruns the irony, like in so much of Daijing's work.

The initial influence on her music comes from outside of music. She has been open about not growing up in a musical household and having very little engagement with the medium in her younger years. She was an avid reader who also engaged with vast amounts of television and cinema. These investigations instigated the spark to think about life and the self in a multitude of ways. It's a fortuitous accident that landed her into the worlds of music, sound, and beyond, giving her the advantage of bypassing imitation and cliche.

A 2015 recording, *A Satin Sight*, is released in 2017 as an EP, leaning far more in the direction of dance music. A tidy sidebar to her other work, this is a classic four-track banger. *Tenderloin Tanz* presents propulsive rhythms that clash for the stereo field as all manner of sonic play shoot around the space. This is Pan Daijing at her most deconstructive of the dancefloor coda. *A Season in Hell* generates a relentless floor kick, finding itself in a competition with an asymmetrical synth snapping away at the core. *A Satin Sight* is an unexpected audio bomb. Daijing has never released anything like it before or since.

The 2017 release *Lack* 惊蛰 unleashes a confident vision where, from the outset, the human voice falls into the sound of a gurgling and sweeping synthesizer. The ensuing recording presents a variety of human and machine interactions where the innate weirdness of the human competes with the inherent weirdness of the machines. Alongside this odd battle, acoustic instrumentation somehow grounds these alien forces, reconciling them with a common base where they can stage their weird dance around each other.

Suggestive track titles displace any comfort in the spectator/listener, as *The Nerve Metre* and *A Situation of Meat* display a fierce symbiosis of the human interacting with artificial flesh. Tropes of the past are wildly contorted into forms of the now. There is a strong scent of the poetic throughout *Lack* 惊蛰, and the battle with machinery seems less fierce. It is almost as if these opposing forces have made peace. Agreeing to move forward, with grace.

"Noise makes me feel most aware of my ears and my mind. Noise is a way for me to remember my roots and to be able to have deep listening."
— Pan Daijing, borshch magazine, 2021

At the height of industrial techno and living in the city which most embodies the movement, her work deliciously eschews the endless repetition of the genre. She does deploy crunching rhythms or heavily processed voices, but does not rely upon them as shapes, as they twist from the non-human to the human and back again. The album *Jade* 玉观音 from 2021 is a landscape saturated with dread, avoiding any cliches or tropes to tie it to any movement. This is less of a macabre dance between soul and machine than a delicate rolling out of the potential fabric that lies between these elements. The voice screams, but it also speaks. An element of mystery is entwined with the dreams of the internal. She has referred to *Jade* 玉观音 *as "something with no statement, no gesture, or purpose."* It is a birth of thoughts, feelings, emotions, patterns. A birth of pure, raw expression, in distressing and traumatic times.

In the opening lines of *The Goat*, she exclaims, "I didn't ask you to stay, but you stayed," laying out a very human sphere to these mechanical forms. It is a softer voice found in *Dictée* (no doubt a reference to the powerful and deeply haunted experimental 1982 novel by Korean American author Theresa Hak Kyung Cha). A wordless voice drifts on top of a menacing string instrument, invoking a world of feeling with no language. It's as beautiful as it is foreboding. *Jade* 玉观音 is a remarkable exploration of the purity of the human interacting with these disgusting tools of our creation.

"I feel opera is a form that worships the idea of music, every medium that's used is in service of the idea of composition. I resonate with this 'submission'[…] to put oneself at the feet of a musical idea, and activate all sources to illustrate that. This is my drive in working with opera."
— Pan Daijing, Red Bull Music Academy, 2018

Daijing works in opera but prefers the term "life play". As an extension of, or branch from, her recorded work she focuses on an exploration as a means of harnessing the powerful potential of the untreated human voice, with its uncanny ability to directly pierce the listener's soul. A tool to tell a tragedy in the abstract, as words and vocal sounds often create a haunting and exquisite cloud of sound.

Inspired at a young age by a friend that was an opera singer, she was confronted with the power of the human voice, its limitations and also the human ability to challenge any inbuilt constraints. One could surmise this reckoning as one of the key goals of her output: confronting and challenging extremes and limitations. There is no pretension to positioning this form within the lineage of the "great composers" but rather the term is deployed as a means of stretching music beyond the experience of sound. It's in the medium of opera where Daijing truly embraces the many thoughts and feelings inside, creating a total experience outside. Why draw a line between life and sound? For Pan Daijing, there is no logic in such thinking.

It was around 600 BC that the Greek Thales stumbled upon electricity when he rubbed amber with silk. The subsequent charge attracted objects and concurrently the discovery of static electricity.

There's a part where the medium of music is irrelevant; it almost feels like the many other forms employed by the artist: photography, design, architecture, video, opera, poetry, and movement are all embraced equally as a means of expressing the mind and spirit. *Tissues* as an album came about through a performance installation of the same name which premiered in the Tanks at Tate Modern in Autumn 2019. In this perfor-mance, all matters of form gently collide to create a symbiotic whole. *Tissues* engaged with the conventions of opera and tragedy to present a searing representation of the embattled human psyche in space and time. While the ambitious multi-sensory artwork made use of the whole range of her artistic capabilities, music, particularly the voice, was at its formal and emotional core. The four parts that comprise the recorded representation of *Tissues* are only an excerpt of the audio which appeared in the live version of this epic work. The fact that it is an excerpt fits elegantly into her reluctance to sit down and consciously "make a new album". The presentation of this audio is simply a byproduct of the greater vision, and as a single element of this whole, it is both innovative and a stand-alone statement overwhelming in its unique construction and ambition to deeply explore these musical thoughts and forms that have been rotating around her soul throughout her practice.

Music of any kind has the unique ability to transform the inner self into sound waves to affect the inner self of others. Recorded or amplified music is unique in its one-to-one transmission of the non-visual thoughts of humans. A direct dialogue from the inner mind to other minds, music resides as a dialogue of the psyche, presented here on the demarcation that separates music from sound.

As the music of Pan Daijing continues to shift through time, it also bleeds into her other forms of exploration. Can the sound of clothing compete with the scent emitted from computer noise? Does light from a projector haunt the wall in which it is embedded? Do arms tangle themselves within the mind that operates them? Does history reside in a "back there"? Or does it endlessly surf within the now? The sheer breadth of her understanding and exploration of the potentiality of music is a long stretch from

Jerry Lee Lewis playing the piano with his foot. It comes from that lineage and shatters it at the same time. She has a natural ability to harness the flow of the self as it exists in real time and space.

Daijing's music presents an ever-evolving expression of her own unique experience. It's a mercurial deployment concocted via machines and thoughts to create something more like a perfume in its ability to attract or repeal. This is a construct where ancient cultures and phantasms dance with demons, personal fears and desires. Unlike Kraftwerk, for instance, the tools deployed are irrelevant to the resulting sound. The tools are merely a means of capturing something that is inside, of presenting the inside to the outside.

Pan Daijing adopts a humble tone, repeatedly asserting her lack of any professional training. The electronic gear is mentioned simply as a means to an end and not spoken of with any vintage "status bravado" that is so often associated with this particular community. When initially mapping out her musical creations, she proudly confesses her ignorance of labels such as experimental, noise, or avant-garde that are applied to her work. As a performer, she displays a deft web of tactics that bypass standard electronic performance and presentation. A backing track is often a mere sound stage that Daijing uses as a platform to improvise in all kinds of manner, voice, movement, speech, and song. It is not uncommon for objects lying in the space to become props or drapes at the back to be incorporated spontaneously as mock stage curtains.

All languages, Western, Eastern, invented language, nonsense language twisted outside of meaning, can make an appearance through her microphone. However, Pan Daijing concedes that she predominantly communicates in English. In her use of language, spoken word magically transforms into song, and back again. The presentation in the live context often involves the use of masks, a tactic deployed to blur identity and bypass judgement in the scene, allowing the work to be. It was only often at the end the audience was made aware this was all concocted and presented by an Asian woman. She can appear wearing a suit, ironically adopting the sartorial codes of the business world. There can be a negated sensuality at play as all these elements entice, entertain, and provoke the spectator. At any time, it can shift from being awkward, charming, and suddenly alarmingly aggressive. A desk of electronic equipment can appear on the stage, which Daijing will then start to operate, plunging the proceedings into a fierce, almost "power electronics"-type set.

There are a couple of anecdotes in particular about Pan Daijing's performances, which illustrate how improvised and spontaneous these live performances of hers can be. When arriving to perform at a festival, gremlins were at play as the sound check only resulted in the unveiling of equipment failure and a non-existent backing track, leaving her with not a single sonic floorboard on which to perform. Whereas most artists would cancel the show in despair, Daijing met the challenge with a relish, even extending the allocated 40-minute set to over an hour of predominantly acappella singing, incorporating elements of games, standup comedy, and strange movements of the body.

The untrained Daijing is a natural improviser, one who can perform with literally nothing but the human psyche and its natural megaphone, the voice. That also goes for anything else, be it a keyboard instrument, or any other instrument: She will find a way to enter into it and extract something which is intrinsically her own. It truly feels like Pan Daijing could make

a compelling live set with only a branch
from a tree. Maybe she is walking out
in front of every house after all. Sousa
would be proud.

Untitled
Series
Since 2012

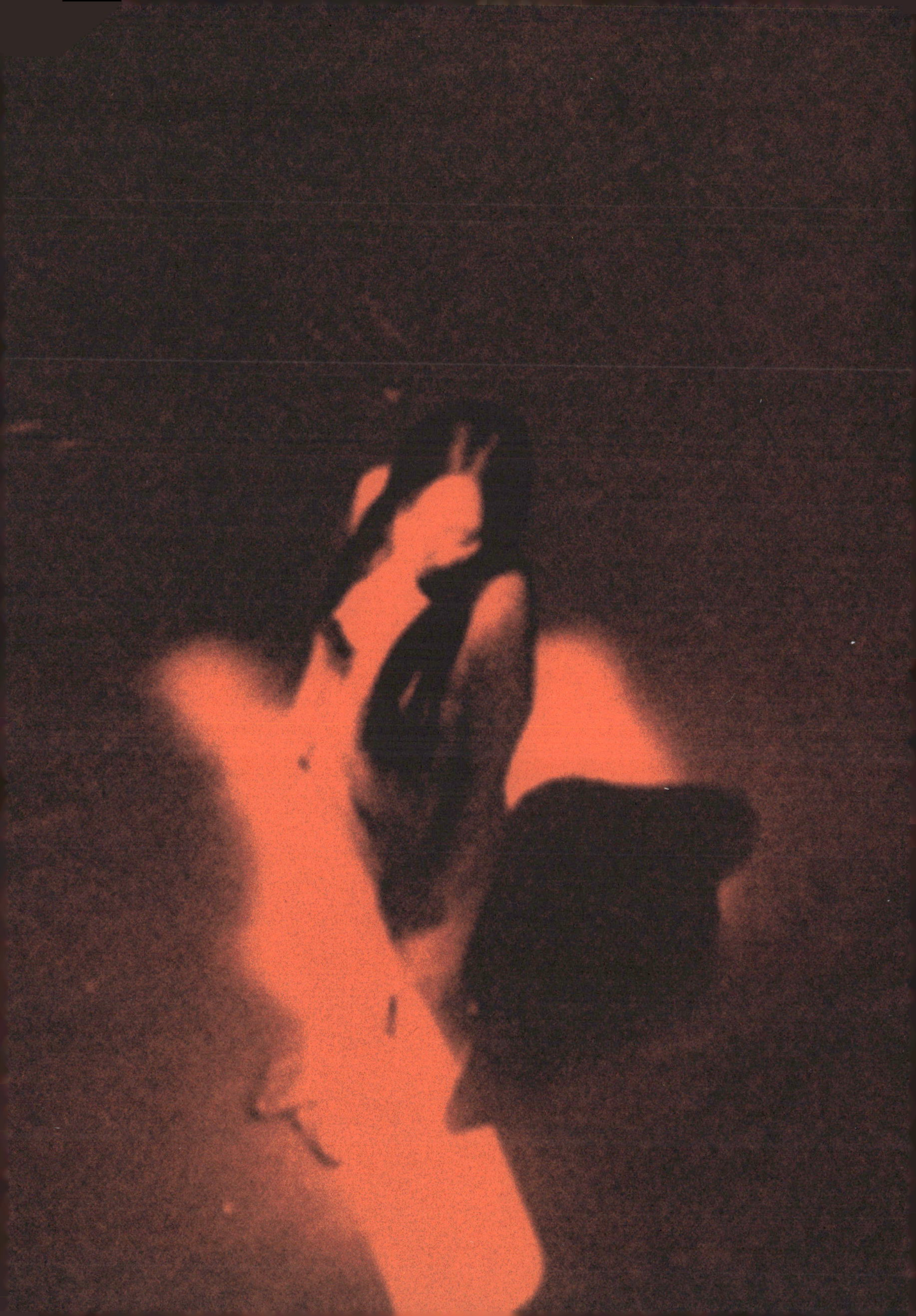

Blank Spaces

This text is a translated and edited version of a conversation between Xue Tan, Senior Curator of Tai Kwun Contemporary, and Pan Daijing, originally held in Mandarin Chinese. The two talk about her solo exhibition *Echoe, Moss and Spill* (16.12.2021–2.1.2022), unspoken truth and interdependence of liveness.

Xue Tan I remember very well our first conversation. We spoke about a Wuxia[1] story set in ancient China, about a young woman swordmaster transforming into a boy. Do you remember?

1 Wuxia translates as "martial heroes". It is a genre of Chinese fiction retelling the adventures of martial artists in ancient China. Originating in literature, Wuxia themes have been adapted for such diverse art forms as opera, comics, TV dramas, films and video games.

XT Could you talk more about that? How did the aesthetics and sound of Hong Kong cinema, as well as the gender fluidity of the characters in Wuxia films and legends from Asia influence you?

Pan Daijing We were talking about the influence of Wong Kar-wai's film *Ashes of Time* (1994) on my work *Tissues*. The story you just mentioned is elaborated in the film *Swordsman II* (1992) with Brigitte Lin in the role of Dongfang Bubai. The Hong Kong directors Tsui Hark and Wong Kar-wai have both adapted characters from Jin Yong's novels and used them in their work. Characters like Dongfang Bubai, Murong Yang, and Murong Yin — they've all made appearances on screen. Growing up and watching Wuxia movies, they had a profound effect on me.

PD It probably has something to do with the environment I grew up in and the repression I experienced in my environment. I found a sense of freedom in these films. I particularly enjoyed watching a genre of Hong Kong films which combines martial arts, legend, and fantasy. They gave me a feeling of being separated from my current reality. Usually tragic, the way these films talked about life's suffering and heroism was directly related to the Chinese society I grew up in—but in the context of a martial arts hero story, with kung fu tactics like "waterwalking" making it possible to transcend the realm of the ordinary without getting lost in superstition.

I like how these stories move between the real and the surreal. Especially interesting to me are the roles played by women, such as Xu Xian in [the TV drama] *New Legend of Madame White Snake* (1992), a male character whom Cecilia Yip interpreted as feminine. The representation of gender in the dramas and films of those decades was truly groundbreaking.

Chinese classical literature often manifests a type of gender fluidity, for example Qu Yuan's long poem *Li Sao* [*The Sorrow of Parting*] (300BC). Contemporary literature is often subject to constraints that have weakened that aspect. When I was growing up, I related to characters like Dongfang Bubai, Murong Yang, and Murong Yin. They projected my values and identity. I want to be able to use what's around me in this same way, as a form of empowerment. It is not just about gender identity but a way of transcending gender. They exist somehow separate from common reality. It's an isolated existence, and it is as if gender and social identity don't matter to them, which strikes me as extremely romantic.

Many people who grew up in China have had ideas about heroism drummed into them, reinforcing a certain concept of a hero, but I don't agree with this. I don't find this heroic sensibility to be connected with others; it only grants power to oneself, and this devotion allows one the pursuit of one's own romantic ideals — towards attaining a certain transcendence in solitude. This is what I can relate to. I was, as a result, very influenced by the abstract and poetic nature of narratives in these films.

I generally don't agree with the mainstream narrative of heroes. I grew up with a lot of political propaganda without ever talking about the pain or other emotions lying underneath. I think that the Chinese language and culture tend to employ rhetoric, abstraction, and poetry: so many ways of alluding to things. Often, what is left unspoken is where true meaning lies. For me, this method of communication through character-making allows much of what is left unspoken to be felt. While growing up and feeling totally alone, these films were like finding someone or something who really understood me.

XT When I listen to your music, it speaks with a realness, and the sound has a relation to pain. The texture of the sounds and music in your works can be perceived as lacerations or wailing. This must come from lived experiences and emotions. Does it have anything to do with the solitude of the Wuxia figures?

PD My creative process isn't directly inspired by anything, so I can't say that Wuxia films were a source of inspiration — instead, the stories gave me the feeling of having someone to confide in. The same thing happens when I'm creating music. It's a very organic process unaffected by other people's stories. It comes completely from the heart, and then, through a very intuitive, intense process, I am able to find my language. Sound and art enable me to articulate my thoughts. Making music is for me a way of searching for something that is absent in my life; it is a desire, a longing. I have to make music because language has limitations. My questions about life, values, and worldviews are expressed through the music I create.

XT Let's go back to the summer of 2021 when you spent several months in Hong Kong for your solo exhibition at Tai Kwun Contemporary. That period marked a return to the Sinophone world after many years abroad. Could you speak more about the influence of the cultural context, landscape, and communities of Hong Kong on your work process? Was there a sense of familiarity? There were a lot of uncertainties; how did you integrate that time, space, and experience into your work?

PD Being in Hong Kong has been very important for my practice, it is still offering material and thoughts to this day. In Hong Kong, it was not only the nature, the everyday living conditions, or my witnessing of all walks of life; it all reminds me a lot of the Chinese city I grew up in, Guiyang — from the mountains and lush green vegetation to the ways that people relate to nature and how the city and nature come together. Guiyang, a city in Southwest China, is described by many as a "little Hong Kong." Guiyang probably has more nature, but the visual impression is very similar to Hong Kong. In contrast, Hong Kong is very capitalistic, like Western countries. For someone like me who has lived in the West for a long time, this cultural mix of East and West is intriguing and familiar.

Growing up, I witnessed many different ways of life, including a range of extremes. Whether those extremes were due to poverty or geographical constraints, they have become pictures inside my head, each one a photographic memory that tugs at my heart. I have witnessed situations like that of a seventy- or eighty-year-old man selling scallions from a basket at the market without a license and city management officers [*chengguan*] beating him. I have often seen the injustice that occurs at the lowest rungs of society, some of which is also because China is a society with no real welfare. In Guizhou, which is a mountainous area with a lot of terraced rice fields, many young people left to work in the city, so the elderly have to take care of the farming at home. Farming is not an easy life.

I ask myself: How can we as humans live together? What does it mean to be human in today's society? On the steep roads of Hong Kong Island, for example, in the market that's visible from the main entrance of Tai Kwun in Central, we often see old people pushing trolley carts and heavy goods. One should, I think, never forget one's roots and where one comes from. Observing life in our society is very important to me. I use the art I create as a release, a means of crying out. It is a way to remind us of the extremes of human existence and suffering, yet it also brings hope and resilience.

In China and other societies in East Asia, our lives are greatly influenced by a philosophy that endorses hard work and endurance and shows great respect for resilience. When I arrived in Hong Kong, I had to be quarantined, which was mentally and physically extremely challenging for me. And then in July we filmed in these claustrophobic spaces, with very high temperatures. I am a sensitive person, and I often challenge my weaknesses through my work.

In the West, my work is experienced differently; in Hong Kong, I feel that people resonate with things in the same way I do. That gives me a lot of creative confidence, and I can be more discreet and metaphorical. I know that people are familiar with poetic and metaphorical communication, and I know that such "blank spaces" can be understood. On the specific occasion of *Echo, Moss and Spill*, I was able to stay until the end of the exhibition. I could observe how my work effectively communicated with the audience, and their feedback was tremendously rewarding to me.

XT The exhibition included an important video work, which you describe as a science fiction film. In this work, we follow a group of people walking together through a vast landscape. From time to time, they engage in intimate encounters, nestling up against one another. They seem independent and interdependent at the same time. They probably know each other — or perhaps they don't — but there is a strong sense of togetherness, like folks "huddling around a warm fire in the face of an apocalypse." Earlier, you spoke about your observations of individuals in society; I know where these sensations and contexts are from. Is this work a reflection of your state of mind in the year of 2021, a response to an uncertain future after the pandemic?

PD "Huddling around a warm fire in the face of an apocalypse" is well put. The work *Moss* is about the apocalypse. COVID was one piece of the picture, even if the work isn't directly related to COVID.

I'm interested in our living environments, how we grow up, especially in Chinese society, as independent but lonely individuals — how do we find hope in solitude, all the while living within this extreme collectivity?

COVID pushed some of these experiences to a global level. Though the reasons may be different, the resistance or resilience against despair, the sheer necessity to find hope in the face of futility about your situation. Even though my work deals with distance, solitude, and the crushing despair, it actually points to possibilities in the search for hope and continuation.

For me, wandering between emptiness and existence, between reality and science fiction, and searching at the extremes — these are important processes. At this time, our living environment is so oversaturated with information, to the point where it's difficult to get a sense of what is real and what is fake. There's too much noise, and the nuances get washed out — like ephemeral moments blown about by the wind. I hope my works can be a call for attention to detail, attention to silence, attention to sensibility. It's possible that during COVID we were more open to our senses because our world became a bit quieter.

XT I would like to talk about how you construct and create realities. The "reality architecture" in the exhibition was arranged very deliberately: a surveillance camera was visibly placed at the entrance. It didn't call attention to itself, as it could have been part of the museum's security system, but it created a livestream of the installation work. After this comes the apocalyptic sci-fi video installation, in which close-ups of the various characters show their facial features and details of their bodies in sharp detail. From there, one steps inside the largest exhibition space — the live performance installation, in which all the characters introduced in the video work are present. The structure you created for these different realities in the exhibition was extraordinary. Is this layered structure — I think of it as a dream within a dream, a play within a play — is it a structure you've experimented with before?

PD I hope all of my works open with this experience of moving through different layers.

Naturally, the structure varies greatly according to the space, because the space is the driving force. What was particularly nice about the building of Tai Kwun Contemporary is that the stairs and three floors can form a progression that starts outside and moves inward.

When I conceived the choreography for the space, I took all of these structural layers into consideration. Some of my previous works, *Tissues* (2019) [at the Tate Modern in London] and *Done Duet* (2021) [at the Power Station of Art in Shanghai], have had this same type of structural arrangement, but not to the same extent as here in Hong Kong, where there is more space to create layers. The live streaming element in *Echo, Moss and Spill* appeared in some of my previous works, too, such as *SEAL*, an installation I did for the *Metabolic Rift* exhibition of the music festival *Atonal* at Kraftwerk in Berlin in 2021. But in Hong Kong, I was able to push this logic to a new depth.

As you mentioned, there was a sense of trust among the performers, which enabled me to indulge in and explore this sense of disorientation. Metaphorically,

XT In the early planning stages of the exhibition, we didn't anticipate that it would have this cumulative process, that it would involve a process of growth and evolution. The performers underwent a particular psychological process during the three weeks of the exhibition. You were present every day as the artist, the performer, and the observer. By the end of the exhibition, words had been drawn all over the walls, transforming the space into a site of emotional and psychological release. Could you share more about how the mental space of the performers changed over time?

it's as though I talk to you about a lake, then I bring you to the lake — and it would feel as though you yourself managed to get there. Then you're left to sit there. This becomes a very special journey. Of course, I have used these dramaturgical methods in previous works, but I wasn't always able to bring them to the level they were in at *Echo, Moss and Spill.*

PD The opportunity to use a space over such a long period of time had never presented itself to me before. Creating the exhibition was a two-part process. At first, I got to know the space and learned to coexist with it. An important element of my practice is that the creative act doesn't end with the opening; it keeps going so that the entire exhibition becomes a continuity of making. As an artist, I was engaged in the process of performance and in the process of observation, seeing how others were engaged. I noticed that a lot of people kept returning to the space many times, and that sometimes when no one was performing, they came in and just wanted to sit in the space to experience the work, while others were hoping to interact with the performers. All of these detailed observations could be thought of as an investigation into the process of making art — which was a precious experience.

In my roles as choreographer and performer, I fine-tune this process of "feeling things out". The exhibition became a lab, a space where I was free to experiment. When I create music, I am constantly posing questions. What was special about this exhibition was that it was

XT Quite often, performers and visitors would interact within the live installation. The work has this open and inclusive nature, embracing and allowing for accidents or mistakes. How does this openness and experimentation differ from your work as an improvisatory musician — is there a similar tolerance towards mistakes and accidents?

XT Could you talk about some of the audience feedback and their influence on the live work?

never still, it was a changing and growing ecosystem, a continuous process, and throughout this process I had the ability to reflect and continuously create, which included the scribbling you mentioned. I let things brew, I let things happen, putting more trust in the process. The exhibition stayed with me, including the scribbles on the walls, and I made more short films and video installations from the exhibition footage. I thought deeply about the project, through observation, during the entire duration. Art institutions are in many ways public gathering spaces, so the question of how to utilise their potential politically and socially is paramount.

PD Yes, this aspect of improvisation is vital, whether I'm creating music or performing. I am a natural born improvisor, improvisation brings the best out of me. Improvisation doesn't mean "spontaneous" or "random", it comes through a long process of reflection and accumulation. It's an organic process.

A metaphor I would use is water: drops of water accumulating in streams and rivers, and through the journey, it forms a magnificent waterfall, pulled by gravity — then it continues to flow onwards and down again. This waterfall wouldn't happen without the initial trickles and the changing altitude. I don't want to control it, because we need that crashing sense of freedom. I long for it; I wait for it.

PD The audience is incredibly important to me. In Hong Kong, I had some conversations with audience members, some of whom came to see the show multiple times. They knew I was the artist and came to talk to me after [that day's performance]. I remember one interaction with a boy: at the time, a strand of my hair fell into his hand, and he later told me,

"This is the heaviest weight I ever held." Ten seconds can feel like ten hours because their impact is so strong. I experienced this myself during concerts when my body turns numb, and there is a sort of outburst. This kind of exchange, I think, is only experienced in person. In my work, these outbursts happen in the most subtle, most insignificant moments, so I have no traces of them through documentation. I need to feel them when they occur, that's why I participate in my performance works.

XT The live work was ephemeral; its appearance was a process over time and only as it was coming to an end, we saw what emerged from it and understood that this was going to stay. For example, I find these scribbles and drawings a unique record reflecting a psychic space of Hong Kong's political and social environment that year.

PD I wanted there to be a personal imprint, whether it's a sound or a poem or a text. I requested each performer to write for about five minutes. When writing, they had to be very discreet, doing their best not to look at the wall. The score was writing the names of all the performers in the space and tracing the fade in and fade out of these moments.

I remember when I was a kid, we played a game called Pen Fairy, a form of automatic writing in which your hand is not in control of what you write. [When I told the performers what I wanted them to do, I would say] "empty your mind, you need a rest, your performance has reached a limit, just let yourself have a go at automatic writing." I gave them this as a score, but I couldn't predict how important the wall drawing would ultimately become. I materialised a key element of my work and preserved an outcome of the improvisation.

XT This is, I feel, a meaningful breakthrough: a collective drawing resulting from a collective process, which is at the same time a true reflection of the creative process. We have talked a lot about the relationship between individuals and collectives, which seems to me a profound element in our upbringing.

PD What I deeply want to express in my works is how we look at social problems and how we reflect on them — yet everyone has to find their way how to address them, so to say. Every society has it's own inherent issues. I have my way of addressing them in my music, artworks,

XT Talking about traces, you've told me quite a lot about your field recordings made in Southwest China. How did those recordings influence your work?

XT Your works deal with intense emotions but you rarely use language to express or even to convey a narrative. What is your relationship with words?

or performances. During *Echo, Moss and Spill*, in Hong Kong, I talked about this with many young local artists or creators. They asked me about it, perhaps because they could sense these layers in my work. I hope to convey that many things reveal themselves only on deeper levels.

PD I enjoy observing all sorts of different cultures. Growing up in Guiyang, the region with the largest number of ethnic minorities in China, I had access to a lot of secluded areas, like the ethnic minorities in Guizhou.

I am not necessarily interested in any specific tradition, but rather how these are passed on. Especially the ways of transmission, the distinctive and mystical oral practice of passing information through generations without writing is fascinating.

And also, how do they find shelter in this extreme natural environment? In the mountainous areas of Guizhou, places can look quite close on the map, but it might take four or five days to drive there. Therefore, music sometimes is the most direct tool for communication. In the end, it is about how people live in what we think of as extreme conditions. In extreme environments, people tend to be very creative and use what they have to make things work. I'm keen to learn from the resilience of people and to find possibilities in impossible situations.

PD Words have a power of their own. How would I put it? Say you're making a bowl of noodles and then you sprinkle a few scallions on top: it's absolutely fine not to add any, and yet, garnish is so important.

I like to use words as hints, as we all have our own interpretations. The process of speculating is the most precious to me, so I hope to focus more on ambiguity and to feel things out in the making. The unspoken is often the most powerful expression.

XT Silence, and more silence.

PD Yes, as Lu Xun[2] said, if you don't break out in silence, you will perish in silence.

[2] Lu Xun (1881–1936) was the leading figure in Chinese modern literature and a revolutionary thinker. He wrote the above phrase in the eulogy of his woman student Liu Hezhen (1904–1926) who died in the March 18 Massacre in 1926, the March 18 protest was considered as one of the earliest student movements in China.

Echo, Moss and Spill

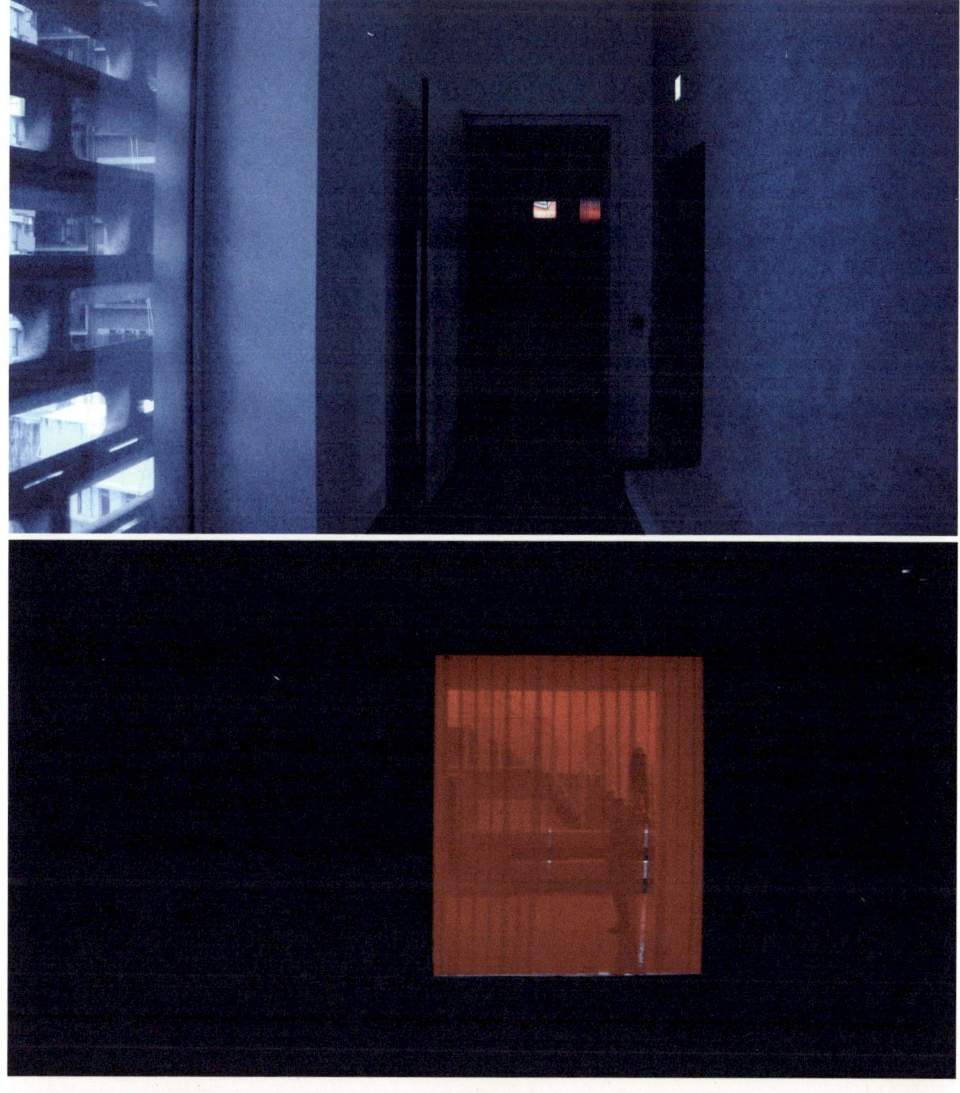

Pan Ling Shu Pak Ting Kwin
Pan Ling Lok Karina Shu Christine Shu

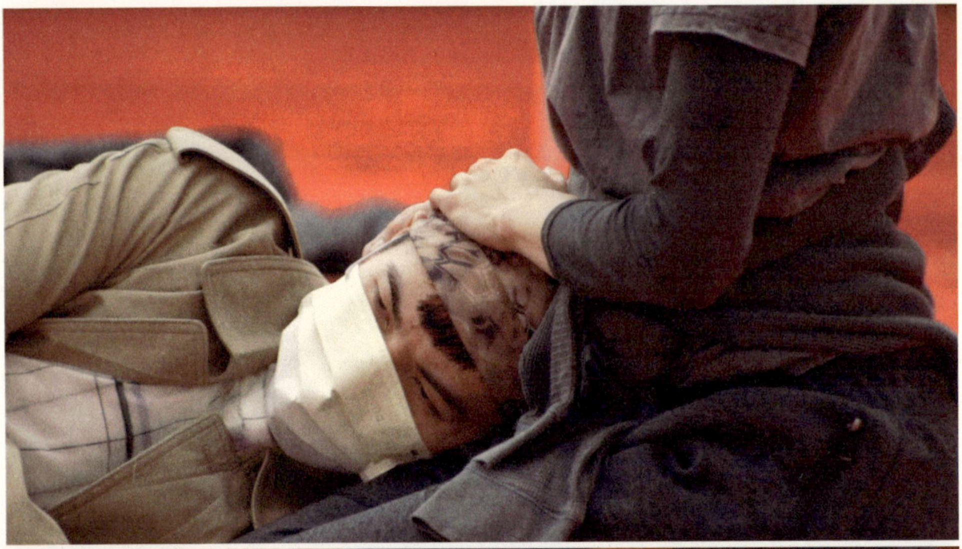

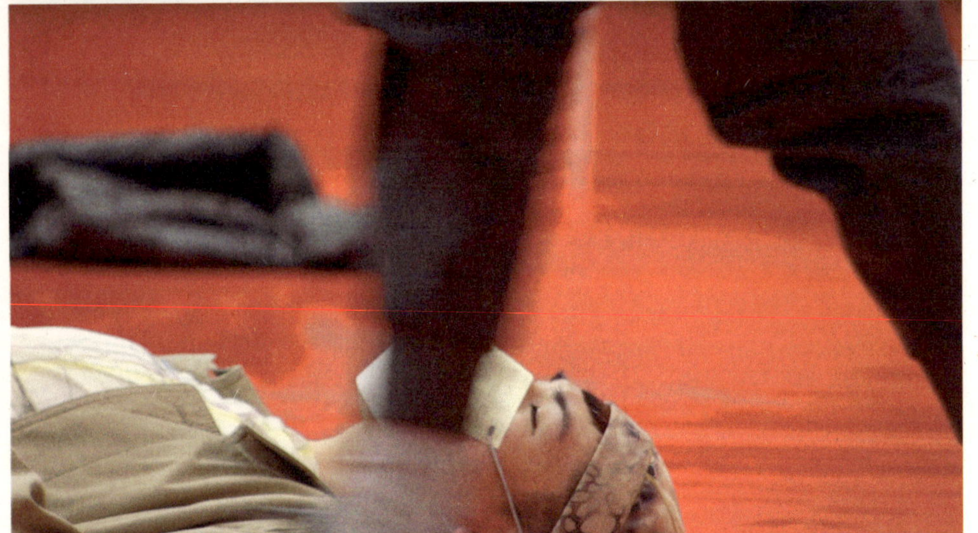

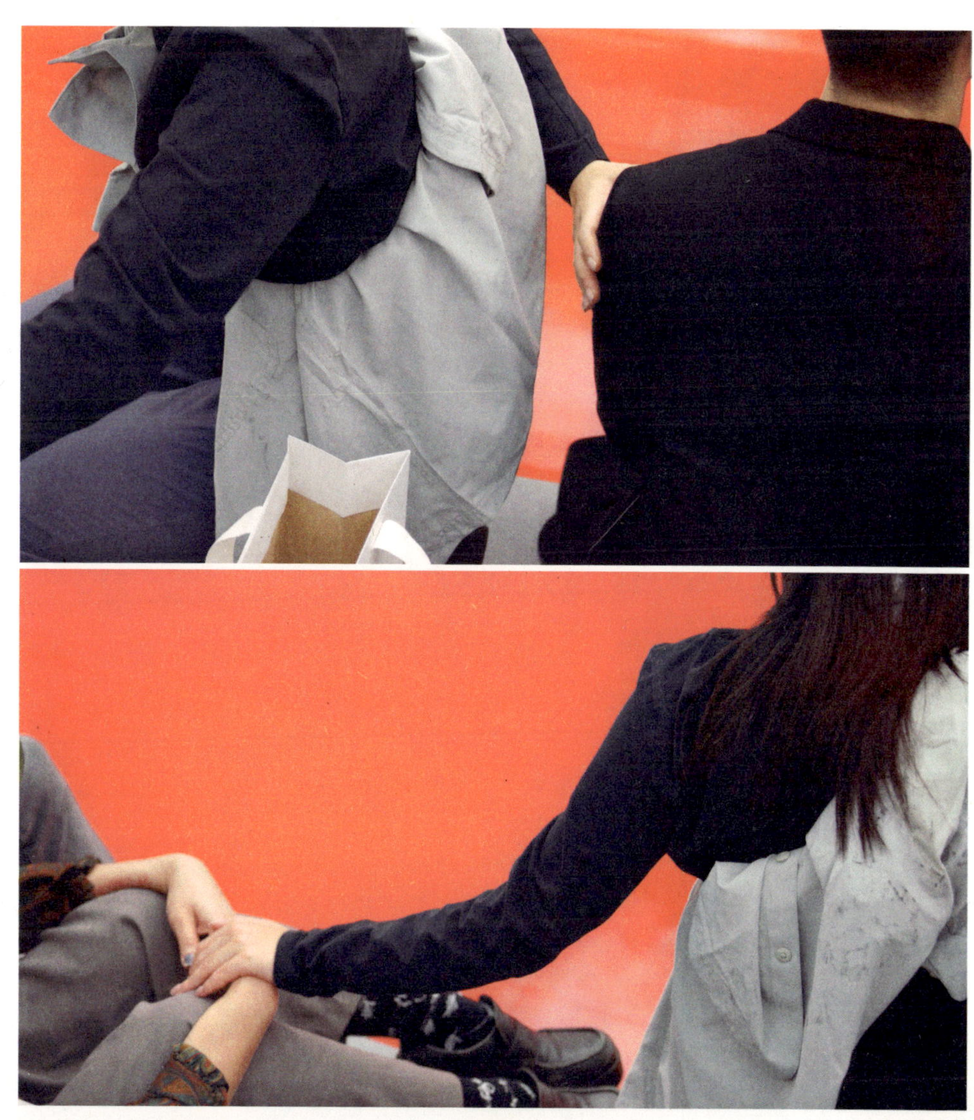

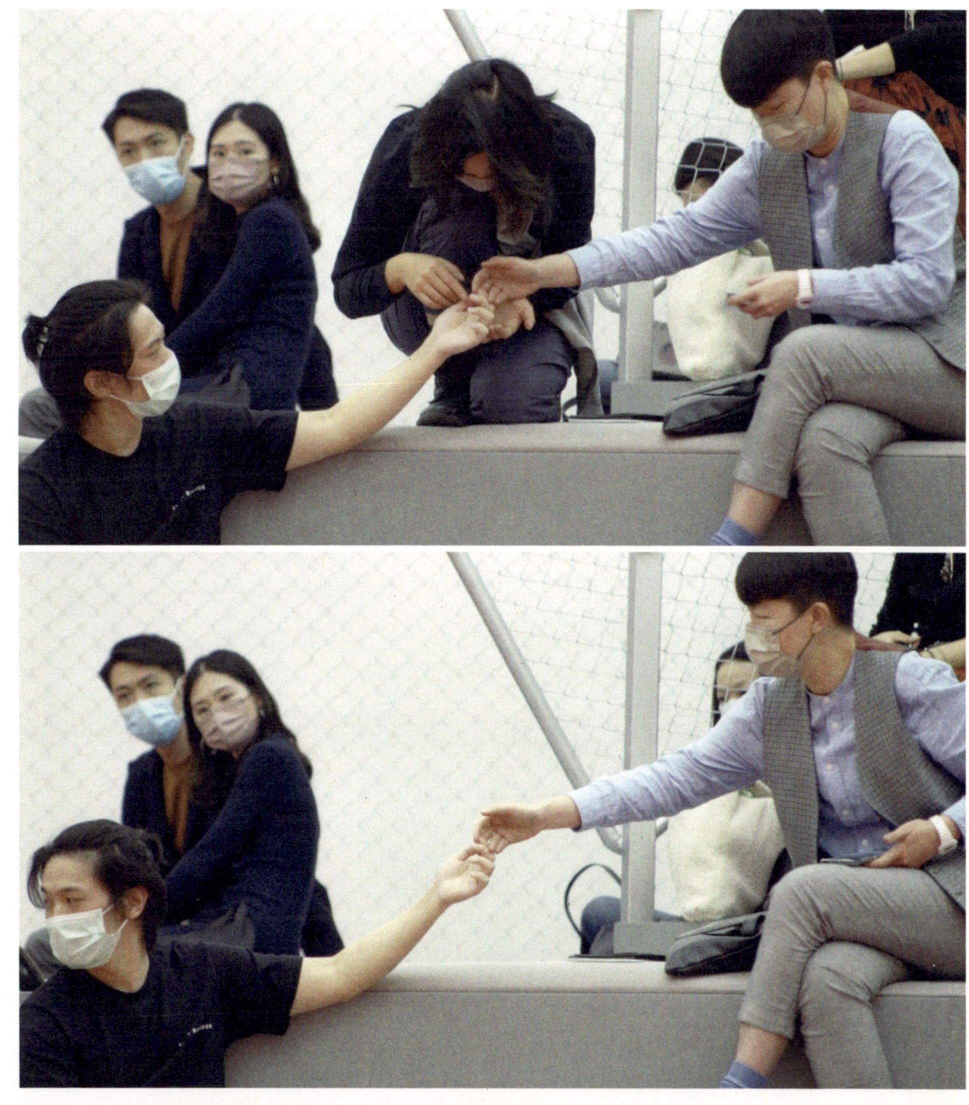

An Offering

This text is an edited version of a conversation between Pan Daijing and Emma Enderby, Chief Curator at Haus der Kunst. In preparation of the exhibition *Mute* (8.3.–14.4.2024) at Haus der Kunst — the artist's largest solo exhibition to date — they talk about scarred and haunted spaces, improvisation, and awe.

Emma Enderby Talking about an exhibition to come is a funny process because we are talking about something that hasn't happened yet. So I imagine people will read this and then have to see the show and wonder what we were on to. But that's the process.

EE So yes, everything we say may not be real.

EE Let's start with the site: the Haus der Kunst Westgalerie. It's a mirror space to the Ostgalerie, which is where we hold our big exhibitions. But it's like the upside down — like a distorted mirror space. It's not perfect, right, the skylights are broken, the walls aren't conditioned in the same way. There are fluctuating temperatures and light tones. I am curious to hear how you reacted when you first came into the space and how the site has guided you towards making the work *Mute*.

Pan Daijing I feel like the exhibition happened a thousand times in my head, but almost every time it is different. I want to be careful with what I reveal because it might change.

PD But I think it's also interesting to see the different stages, to expose the process — will there ever be a result?

PD It's really amazing to work with the space. But it was definitely not love at first sight. The first time I encountered it was difficult, because it's not the kind of space that you can just "have a look at" — it's not just one encounter — it has so many layers and it is actually very dynamic. Everything seems determined by elements outside of the space: what time you're entering, what's happening there at the moment… It didn't immediately resonate with what I had imagined. But as I started coming more often the space revealed itself to me in different ways and I was able to approach the building in a romantic way. I often work with large spaces, in which the architecture already has a loud voice. I feel taken by it. I imagine the space like a challenging lover. I make an effort to understand the beauty of it, and I am humbled by it. The way you described the Westgalerie as a twin to the Ostgalerie resonates with the fact that I am working in the under-dressed, outsider version of the exhibition space. It is more raw, more beat, it's distorted. And that really resonates with me and how I feel as a person. I'm not dressing or polishing the room. It's not about my work occupying a space; the space is the work. I spent a lot of time looking at architectural renderings but also in the space, exploring the basement, the roof, the woods around the museum… All of it helped me to understand the space as a person with a history: what has it witnessed over the years? What's its body like? How much weight has it been carrying?

EE The Westgalerie has its scars. You see them, and you feel them. It can be a difficult space, because it's not stable — normally with the white cube gallery space the condition is stability. Whereas here, slight things change, be it the time of day, or as you said the season, and the whole thing gets thrown. As you noted, it's completely connected and dependent on what's outside the building, as well. It's interesting that you talk about the space being a person. You also once described it as an "overall musical instrument." Which connects to the idea of the body as an instrument. The actual exhibition also begins outside the space, even outside HDK; it's a journey.

PD What interests me in architectural intervention is how we as bodies are able to merge with something that is larger than ourselves. I seek this kind of disorienting experience. Curiosity and excitement both relate to this feeling of uncertainty, which is also how I feel most of the time in life. I think for example the moment you realise the walls of a room may be a skeleton, an unrevealed opening, rather than a barrier.

I refer to this as zoom: zooming in and zooming out. Sometimes, the scale of a building can be intimidating, but come to think of it, we're not intimidated by the size of forests. When you walk into an empty building you might feel intimidated, because you see the border. With *Mute*, I want to expand the building; I want to suggest that what we see is not necessarily the end; there are no borders to the space. Of course, this expansion comes from our imagination, and it could be an illusion. I want to create this sense of safety, of closeness, that you might feel in the forest, that makes you willing to go a little bit further into uncertainty. In my work, it's often not clear what is being presented. I am not interested in the wall as a backdrop or frame—I want everyone to find their own viewpoint. As the artist, I make an offering, but I am not telling anyone where to look. I want *Mute* to be a public space, to be like a forest, a space that one could inhabit. And I should clarify this is not about being comfortable but about a sense of belonging.

This can be a very individual experience. For me, belonging often has a sad undertone. I call this "collective solitude". With my performers, we're talking a lot about the idea of the gathering, which means being independent but in relation. This connects to my philosophy of improvisation.

Although *Mute* extends over many spaces, I don't envision a certain route for it. Some people might walk through all rooms and experience a physical journey through space, others might prefer

EE You are blurring the boundaries. Of course, the blurring between the inside and the outside happens because the space isn't fixed. But in your work, there is also this blur with the notion of mediums… Sound could be sculpture, the building can be an instrument, some of the objects are performative, drawings are performances. You are constantly blurring this idea of what the work can be, which is reflected in the space that is as much part of the show and the work as the objects that you're bringing into it.

EE I don't make art, but I know exactly what you mean; it's that intuitive moment. Making the music for *Mute*, you hadn't thought of the sound before you came to the space, right? Did you have a visual language or world playing out for you when you were crafting it? It seems very interconnected. How do you make the sound for *Mute*?

to be stationary and have a journey inward. I cannot predict how people are being taken by this encounter — and this is beautiful to me. I wouldn't say I'm an expert at playing any musical instrument. But I think the idea of an instrument is that it can be simply played. There is no one way to play. This is how I work like at Haus der Kunst. There are countless ways to activate it. And I am an improviser playing that instrument.

PD The definition of a genre is not important to me. I was never trained in anything I do. So, in a way, doing is the way to define something. For example, when I compose, I just "do" and wait for this click to happen in my head. It requires a lot of preparation to make sure when that click happens, it's clear.

We often have to address an idea with words. But I do believe that the work would speak for itself. One shouldn't be biased about what the instrument should sound like or how it should be played. I compose space and music, I choreograph movement and materials; they all are, in a way, no different than sound. If we look at it this way, it's so obvious that the medium should be blurred. It's experimental storytelling. For example, a video is a video, but if I zoom out to see the video in the space, it becomes a fragment of a choreography. Placing a video is not different from choreographing movements.

PD If I see a movement, that's kind of music and at the same time, when I write music I see something in my head. So the visual and the sonic are never separated but amplify each other. I just love the feeling of being humbled by something that's larger than ourselves; be it nature, be it music. Very often I feel I'm not creating, I'm just revealing what my artistic filter detects in this ocean of possibilities. Space to me is not dead, it's never still. It's just that we as humans don't see it moving. I create a moving landscape to reveal how the space could be alive, like a sleeping monster. A wall might be a concrete surface, but what's behind it, we don't know. Nothing is ever still; everything is always in motion, changing, and I find hope in this. Filming helps me to grasp this motion.

From the very beginning of our conversation we were talking about this idea of the survey. So, I wouldn't say I write the music for *Mute* specifically for the space. I've spent many years working with opera voices, composing, recording and treating them and I am now trying to select from these materials that express how I feel about the building. I'm trying to make a dance with the space rather than placing a piece of music there. It should sound as if the space itself is playing it.

EE You mention the survey, and it's true the show includes objects that you've shown before, or not even objects but relics of performances. And then there's remnants that are left behind from the opening performance that grow through the run of the exhibition. It is a twist on the traditional idea of a survey.

PD A survey is looking back, but here we are looking back at something that's almost ungraspable. I mean — what are we looking at? What's left? It's a huge privilege to look back at these moments and experiences and reassemble those feelings, those memories through familiar or unfamiliar appearances. *Mute* should feel like a déjà-vu. It's an invocation of scores, which is the spirit of past work. It introduces the idea of hope again; although many people think my work is related to pain and trauma, what I'm trying to project is this radiating hope.

EE I think liveness can *be* hope. The way you've treated the space, for me, is also akin to jamais-vu, which is the opposite of déjà-vu, where familiarity suddenly feels unfamiliar or strange. And then there's also the déjà-vu feeling, as you are bringing in materials from the basement, like the old slabs of marble flooring. We've talked about Mark Fisher and hauntology, this idea of a kind of persistent ghosting or returning that exists in a space like Haus der Kunst and is really prevalent in *Mute*.

EE *Mute* might open a crack that one can choose to push further open and transform — or not. During the run of the show, the performers introduce different moments of intensity and rhythms. Do you see them as extensions of the building? How do you interpret these physical bodies within this environment that you're making?

EE How choreographed versus improvised is the performance? Do you give instructions, or how much do you control the performance? How much freedom do the performers have to respond to different triggers or modes or to the audience members?

PD Unfamiliarity is eerie. We can think about this both from a psychoanalytic and a spiritual angle. The world we're living in right now has a lot to do with our relationship with ourselves. I think we often neglect the uncomfortable, the eerie within ourselves, we have very little means to accept, confront, or allow access to all those things within ourselves, the individual self but also society. If we become more comfortable with our own unfamiliarity, for example, through the experience of art and music, we may be able to find means of transformation.

PD I always think in metaphors that put the performers in relation to the larger landscape. The music would be the sky and the building itself the land, the environment I'm building is what's on the land, and the performers shift, everytime they are something different. They could be a passing train or a kite flying in the sky. In *Mute*, I see them as a metronome, as the invisible rhythm of life.

Their movements will be subtle, asking for patience. The choreography is centered around emotional bonds that we form with ourselves and with others: the temperature of skin, the closeness of bodies… But the performers are not the center of attention, not the focus of the experience. All members of the audience are also bodies in the space as they stand in each other's landscape. So they become part of something bigger.

PD This is a big question — what is improvisation?

I don't usually use the word control, because the goal is to let go, but at the same time my choreographies are very strictly scored. My way of choreographing focuses a lot on studying and observing the performers and finding their limits. I'm the conductor, and I conduct the ensemble through my movements. I don't introduce rules, but during rehearsal we all develop some sort of "micro-habits" that allows everyone to go to their vulnerable places. And through this, the performers really become the work. It's much more than performing a work for someone. I always have a very long audition process because it's important that the performers are echoing with the voice of the work. I am very grateful to have always found people who are willing to embark on this emotional journey with me.

Through the exhibition, the philosophy of improvisation will allow us to observe a natural process, which eventually illustrates why the duration of an exhibition and the process of breeding in this environment feeds into the works that come after. If the choreography was scripted in a more narrative way, I'd lose this feeling of uncertainty, and the audience's reaction to it. Observing and studying it allows me to generate new work and I feel I need to hold on to all of these very sensitive details.

EE You say the performers are the work, but you are the work, too. There's your own constant rethinking and reevaluating and the fluidity that comes from that. When you were talking, it made me think of your last show in Graz and the relationship between the performance and the videos in your work. At first, the videos felt like individual works and suddenly they all connected, visually. When they synchronised, I understood that there's this duality playing between the individual image and how they are part of the network. And this relates so much to the way that you make your shows and your environments because, going back to what you said earlier, it's always an individual experience, but it's nested within this collective framework or feeling. That goes for the audiences but also for the relationships of the performers as well.

PD This moment of synchronisation, for me, is the voice of the work calling. In *Until Due Time Everything Is Else*, it was a light coming through the clouds, piercing through all the layers. I remember twelve years ago, I was sitting in a Tibetan temple. Through the sound of horns and chanting, I had intense visions. I was flowing in this dark hole and suddenly the sound of a bell drags me back, making me solid again. My inspiration and my methods draw on first-hand experience, and this specific experience inspired me to study this "calling", this moment of synchronisation that brings us together, somehow reassuring our existence, and allowing us to go to a brighter or darker place, together. It will continue to happen in *Mute*.

Uncut

Done Duet

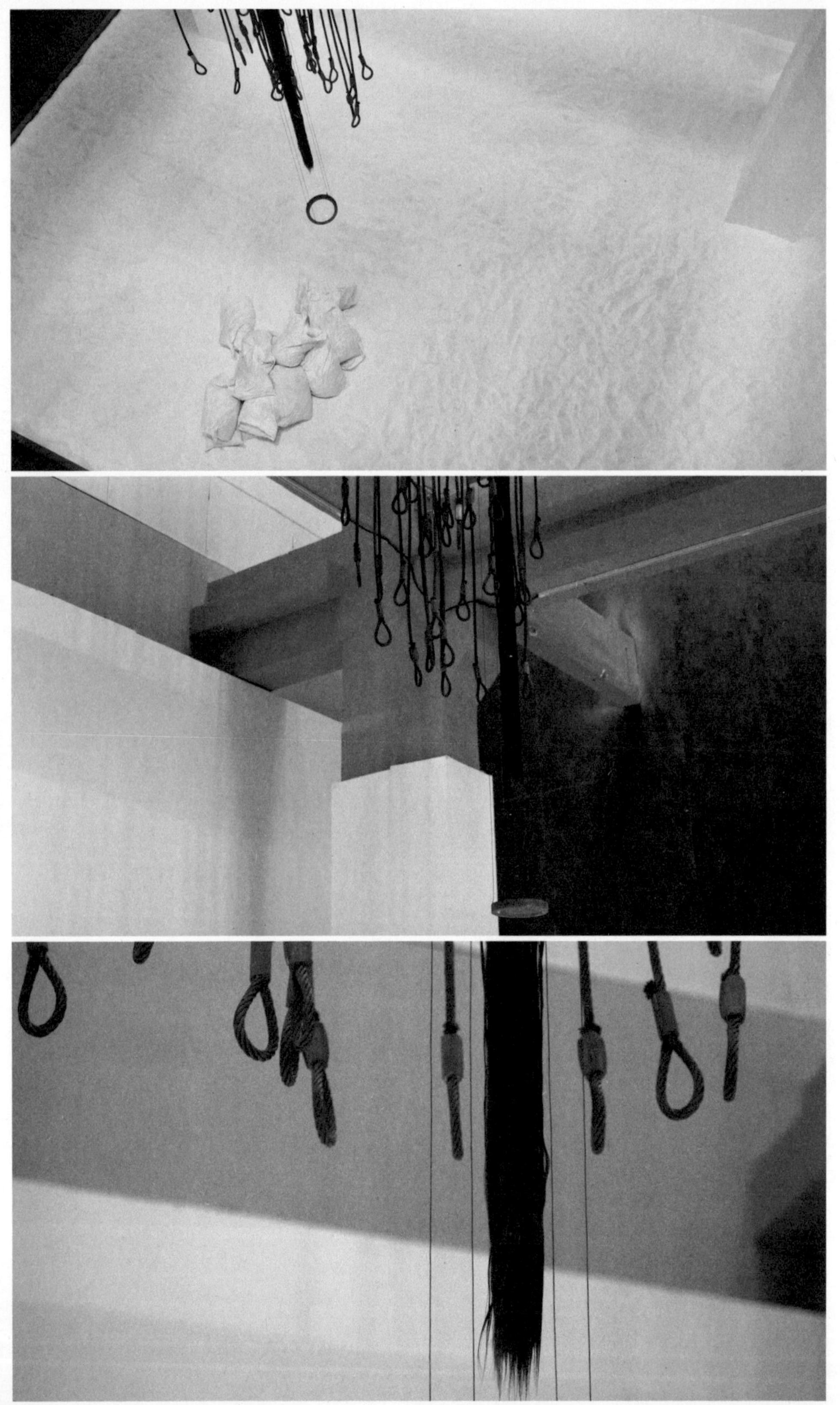

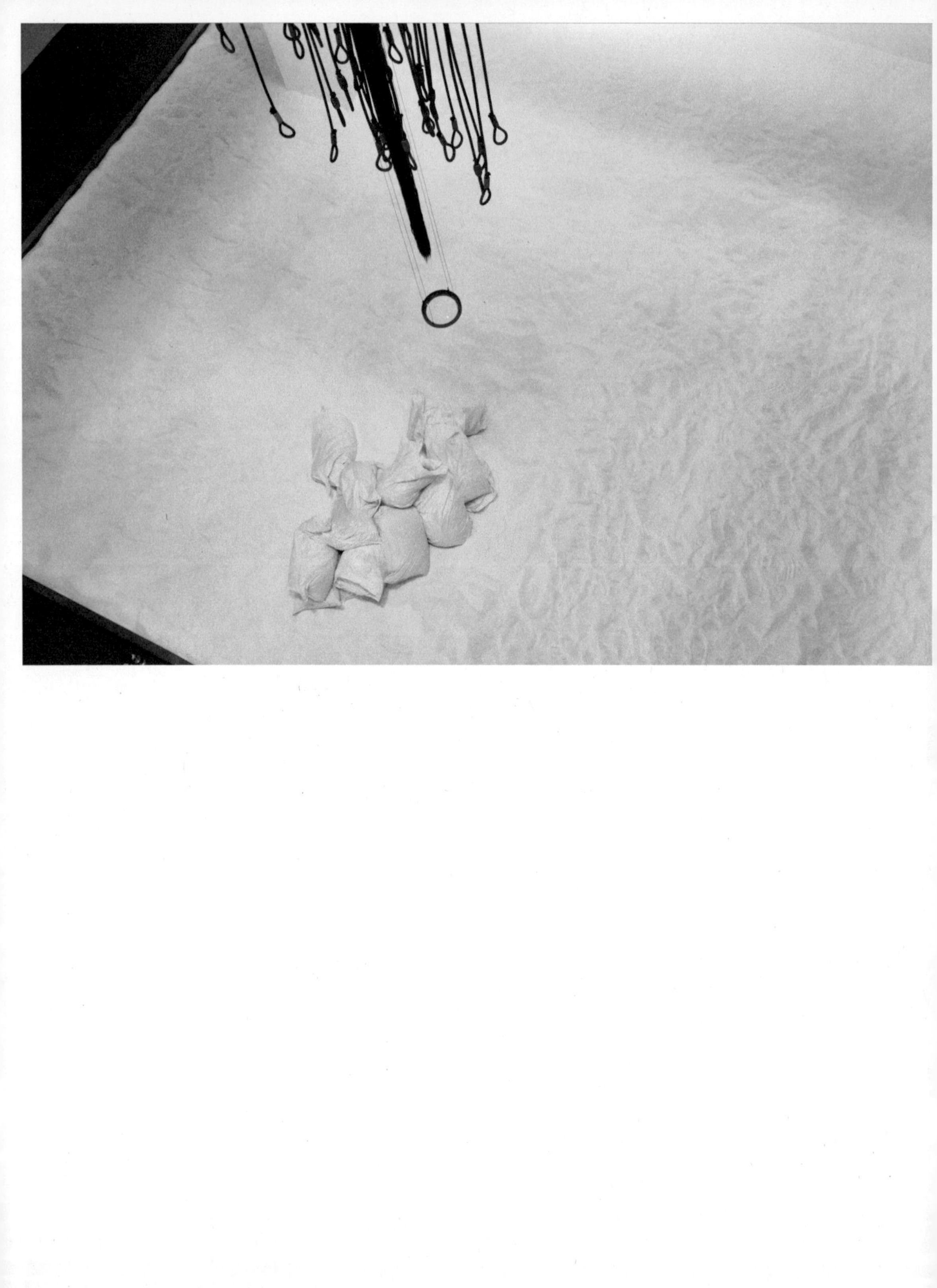

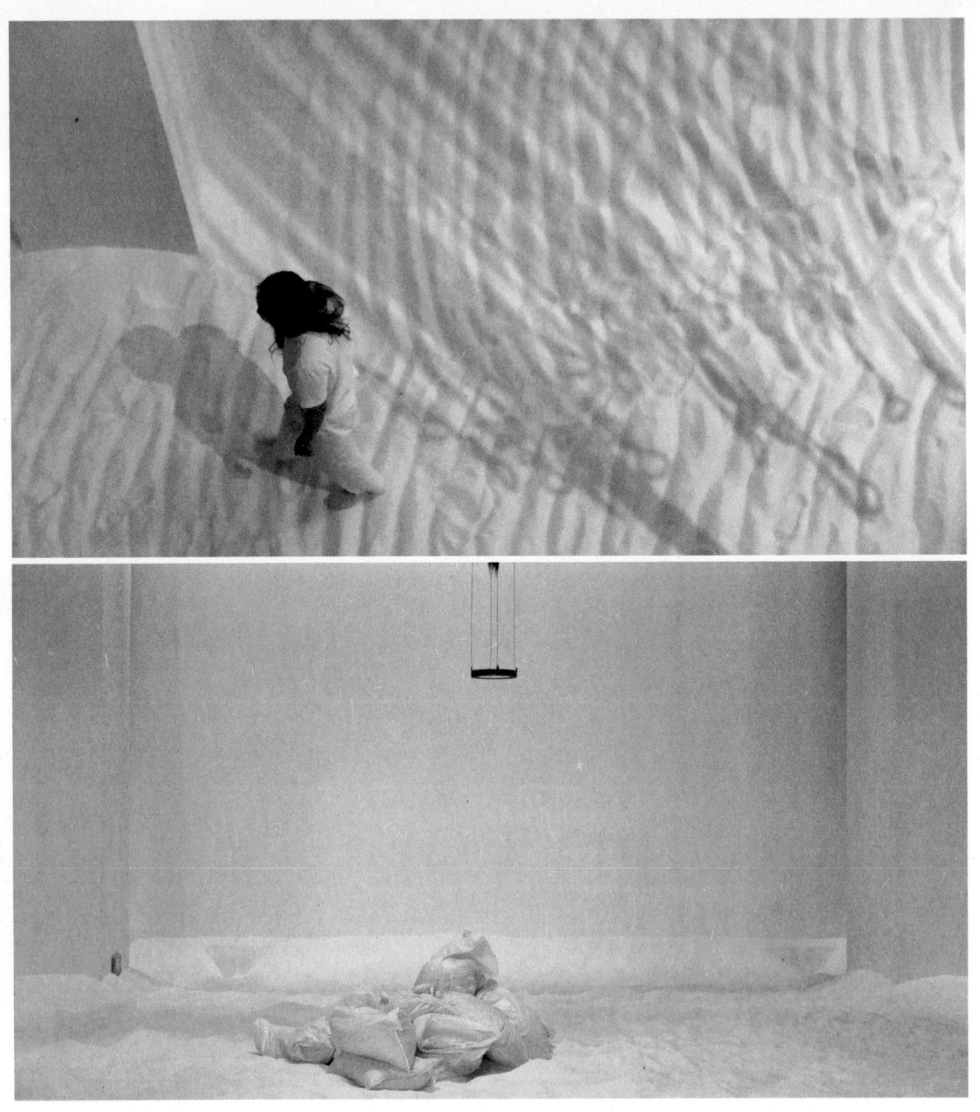

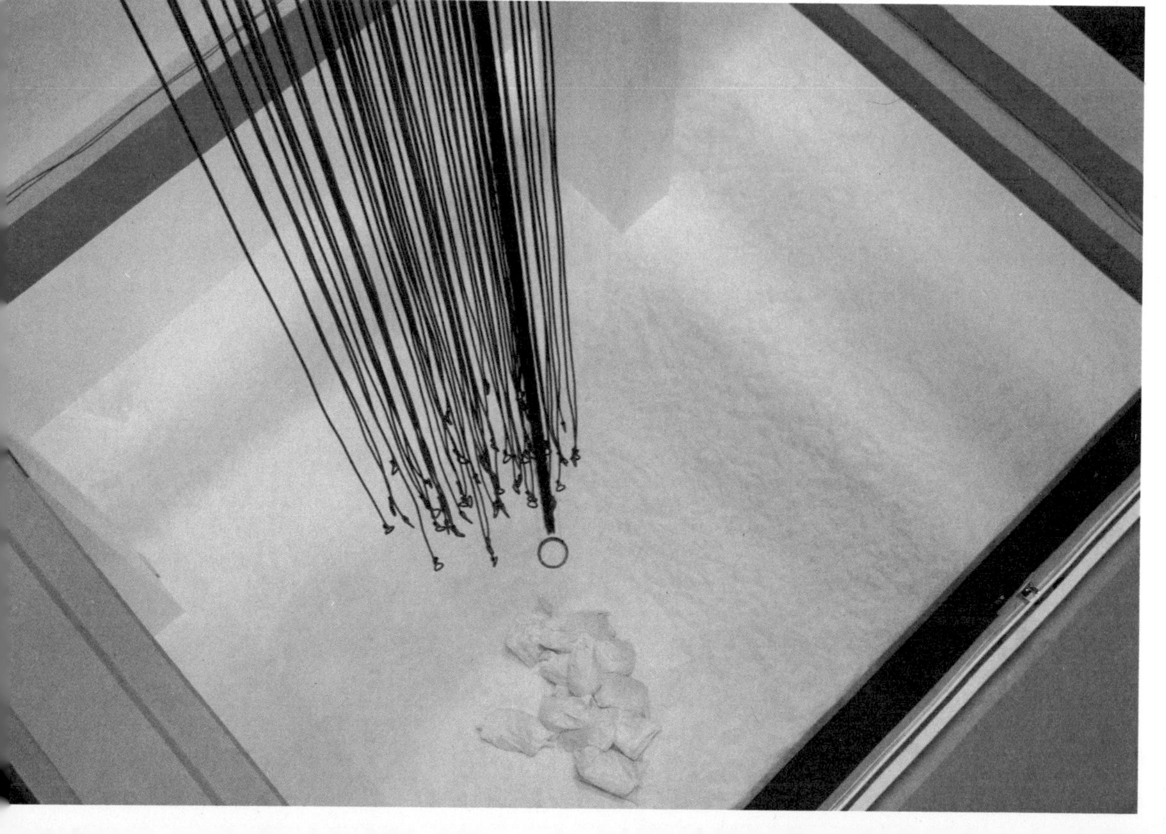

Sarah Johanna Theurer
Morphic Traits

Pan Daijing's work can never be experienced from a safe distance but only through an embodied experience. Sound, light, temperature, and all the small, almost imperceptible transitions of her choreographies operate primarily on the peripheries of perception. I might never fully comprehend the works–but I can feel them living inside me. The works' propositions are paradoxical: rooms appear, at once, empty and filled; encounters tend to be intimate and alienating at the same time. Although often described in terms of performance, her work is neither concerned with presentation nor is it concerned with the nostalgias of process and documentation. I like to think of her work as a fabric of overlapping sequential and synchronous processes or as rich and opaque transmissions.

The work's natural habitat is the grey zone between exhibition and performanceinstallation: Daijing initially assesses a given space, then activates it by accentuating its qualities through the addition of light and sound. This sense of motion results from the fact that we see the space twice: first as we experience it in "real life", then as it is recoded in her work. Her treatment energetically charges the space and makes it responsive. The relations between all elements that compose these environments are dynamic, entangled in a rhythmical composition. It is a kind of art that requires a break of routinised forms of perception: suspension of disbelief, as in theatre, or a desire for aesthetic estrangement. Only this will allow the work to temporarily substitute for and partially integrate into the "real world". Great care and attention is put into creating this reality distortion field.

The seed of a work might be an image, a smell, a sound or a story stretched out into three-dimensional space, distributed into discrete moments, or dissolved into an atmosphere, temporarily held together by the carefully choreographed triangulation of artist/conductor, space/container, and the witnessing bodies. The kernel expands into the witnesses' minds, where it replicates and lives on as memories, plant-like, each idea stemming from the same root but with leaves coloured in different shades of personal interpretation. Such work may be fragile, but it's not frail. "The work" (I want to use quotation marks here, contesting any claim for unity and completeness) operates across multiple dimensions simultaneously; in the moment in which it manifests itself, it simultaneously morphs into another form and is distilled into a memory or a film, a photograph, another idea, another constellation of still and moving images. Morphing is an effect that sees one shape transform into another in a seamless transition. It's a gradual process, now often used to describe the special effects of cinematic animation. This is why it seems so fitting a term for Daijing's work, which engages and challenges animation and liveness.

While these morphic traits are not magic, they are definitely more magical than the classical model of broadcaster / receiver, which has governed both the exhibition and the event space for a long time. Because of its morphic traits, the work cannot be captured; it is best approached through metaphor, something that stands in for what one can see or hear but cannot obtain. The essential ingredients can be condensed into a recipe, but, like a meal, it will always have to be made anew; the acts will have to be adapted to what's at hand and how many participate in the feast. As the work morphs, whether by itself, by the artist's hand, or by the time of day, it also affects its surroundings.

For Pan Daijing, every work is less a discrete object or isolated instance but rather a moment, linked backwards and forwards to others. This thought was lingering in my mind as I stepped into the hazy atrium of Berlin's Martin Gropius Bau in 2020, where a friend of mine performed in Daijing's *Dead Time Blue*. Just a few months earlier, I had been at the premiere of her opera *Tissues* in London, and its impressions were still resonating within me. The individual performer had been dissolved in a meshwork of tones, voice, space, and instrument, all existing in both consonance and dissonance with each other. Now, in Berlin, I was carried by the awe of anticipation and relieved to re-encounter traces of the previous piece and its protagonists. In my head, both works built on each other in a seamless continuation, pre-image and after-image, forming a mesmerising landscape filled with disembodied and live opera voices.

Daijing often refers to her compositions and choreographies in terms of landscape. This word, in particular, has denoted very different things throughout the changing histories of art. It was only recently that I found the term "landscape dramaturgy" in Ana Vujanović's essay *Meandering Together*, from 2017. Vujanović ties the notion to Gertrude Stein's concept of the "landscape play", where the landscape on stage has nothing to do with the natural landscape but rather with the principles of collage and montage as introduced in the cinema and visual arts of Stein's time. Repetition, multiplication, and simultaneity are all narrative tools that we find in Daijing's performances and videos. Timing is one possible key to connecting to her choreographies. But, as the artist herself has often stressed, these efforts are merely supporting acts for what Susan Sontag calls the "hallucinatory detail". Any driving action, voice, or movement could suddenly retreat into the background in favour of an off-centre detail that catches the artist's attention. Reaching into cinema's lexicon, Daijing characterises this strategy as "zooming in". This inverse relationship of landscape and figure is what links Vujanović's landscape dramaturgy to Daijing's endeavour. The idea of a work that I am part of, that I cannot measure except with my own senses, that turns me, whether performer or audience member, from the figure in the foreground into a detail among other objects in the landscape.

Aside from the collective moments of arrival and exit, the audience is free to organise their space-time during the performances. All performers are present, but their attention is turned inwards as if they were unaware of being watched. Long shots and distant views are reproduced through light that tenderly frames silhouettes and cast long shadows. The scene might seem undetermined, and everything may appear to be of equal importance. We witness her works as an assortment of differently paced micro-events and seemingly inconsequential actions: interruptions, transitions, intervals, in-between moments. The audience isn't being told where to look.

There are usually no metatexts in her work; neither wall texts nor pamphlets containing "must-have" info to arrest shallow attention. Moving among the performers, the artist observes the different levels of uncertainty rising in those present. One must take in everything, every tiny detail. However, it is usually not possible to see or hear all the materials created by the performers because other people are around and obstruct one's gaze or because several scenes are happening simultaneously. And, while everyone has their own individual view, there is always a whole that no one can witness. This is not unlike the ways we experience the "real" or "immediate" world outside of the artwork, which, constantly shaken by unthinkable disasters, becomes increasingly difficult to comprehend.

Indeed, moving through the landscape of Daijing's work is quite similar to doom-scrolling: there is uncanniness, concurrent with a certain collective jouissance in the mesmerised contemplation of "The End Of It All"; the feeling of being doomed, of always being too late, for the end has already happened many times.

Her work exudes a deep distrust in the organisation of the world. And this fuels its morphic traits and activates its reality distortion field. "The only way to situate ourselves as an audience in this world [the artwork] is to enter as one of the components of that unstructured world, to meander through it together with performers and other audience members," as Vujanović puts it. Ever so slightly, the work morphs the audience's perception. By tempting the audience members to position themselves within the landscape, Daijing's choreographies suspend the perspectival order that constructs the landscape from the position of the first-person singular. Instead, she introduces an impersonal view. Perspective creates reality. Perspective is how we approach or "think" the world. The result of the first-person singular perspective is individualism and anthropocentrism. Within the artwork's reality distortion field, these modes are relinquished in favour of an impersonal perspective.

One biography of Pan Daijing states that the artist is "[...] seeking a means of connection beyond the human condition". Eugene Thacker, whose resourceful philosophical exploration of horror is my guide to the borders of the human condition, writes: "While we can never experience the world-in-itself, we seem to be almost fatalistically drawn to it, perhaps as a limit that defines who we are as human beings." Anxiety and fear are an important part of that definition, and Daijing knows this all too well. Her work is often perceived as gloomy and haunting. This is apparent in her dedication to nuanced dissonance in music, to rumbling electronics and mourning voices, to droopy tone-in-tone fabrics and dimly lit spaces. On a dramaturgical level, the effect of doom is created through the compositional / choreographic role of the landscape and the device of impersonal perspective. This detached way of experiencing is deeply disorienting and requires far more than an embrace of aesthetic estrangement or the suspension of disbelief. Of course, these are still needed because, as noted earlier, we are all part of the landscape; nobody ever witnesses the whole. The work remains hidden in plain sight.

Nevertheless, it's undoubtedly there, here and now, and it requires everyone to reorient in relation to its unstructured world — one in which there is no barrier to demarcate or mediate between that which Thacker calls the "world-in-itself" and what Vujanović refers to as the "thingness of the world" — and the immediate reality, which we can perceive with our sensory faculties. Accepting to be part of something that one cannot comprehend equals accepting to be doomed. However, if doom is a dominant condition, it may become generative, a beginning rather than an end. Surrendering, one might gain acuity of perception and develop new sensitivities or supernatural capacities. By giving up the magic circle of the stage, the performance score, and even the hierarchical order of gaze, her work amplifies the blurriness of the individual and that which lies beyond it, reaching for a different kind of connection to the world.

Her quest for connection is not just social. Early on, she invites other-than-human agents into play. The streetlights in front of the Pavillon Sicli in Geneva had a key role in her ensemble of performers for *Tissues I: A Prologue* (2018). Her pet — a tortoise — starred in the performance *In Service of a Song* (2017 / 18). Since reality is constructed by our sensory faculties, the world as inhabited by a human being does not only look or feel different; it *is* different from the world inhabited by, for example, the tortoise. Here I quote from the artist's statement on the work *In Service of a Song*:

> [...] a musical work without sound. It invites the viewer to experience the possibilities of sonic imagination. Four improvised performances, each lasting thirteen minutes, took place on consecutive days inside a soundproofed installation. Surrounded and filled to ankle height with soil, the structure appeared to have forced its way into the building through the floor, like a plant growing through a crack in the concrete. Inside this installation [...] the artist was joined by an array of sculptures [...] and her own tortoise, the only living organism to witness the performance from inside.

As the audience circulates the perspex shed in which the artist moves and sings for and with her tortoise, their shifting views destabilise a clearly displayed ground. This multiplicity of perspectives will later be highlighted in an installation of the same work that includes four videos that capture the performance event from different angles. For the audience outside the box, the only stimulus accessible is the visual strata. As described by the artist, it generates hallucinatory details of the auditory elements. The tortoise stands for a radically different perspective on the same event: The animal is known to be incredibly sensitive to vibration, hearing only the sound frequency range between 50 and 1000 Hz. What is on display in the perspex shed is that which lies beyond human comprehension. And notably, this is not the horror of the unhuman or the supernatural. It's just another nature. And according to Pan Daijing, it is music.

In chronological terms, *In Service of a Song* is the forerunner in a series of experiments in how we navigate through a world that is not there for us alone and how we, as humans, inscribe ourselves within it. The reality distortion field of her work makes it possible — or necessary — to coexist with the world-in-itself. *In Service of a Song* reminds us of the coexistence of myriad ways of perceiving the real. Adding another element to her bodily sensorium, Daijing often records her surroundings with a handheld video camera. Even during her own music performances, she records her audience. Her work consists primarily of affects and experiences — not only concepts, technical riders, or musical scores. She records her audience because she is looking for patterns that systematise experience, theirs and hers. During rehearsals, she would sometimes revisit these patterns with each performer individually and relentlessly. The observations of affects emanate into poetic gestures such as *Footnote* (2023), a mix of bone meal and volcano powder dried up dripping from the wall at Grazer Kunstverein. It suggests that the walls have been sweating, oozing struggle or desire in reaction to something they have witnessed. The seven drops resemble the seven notes of the major scale, pulled down the wall by gravity; their shape is a manifestation of uncertainty. The writer Carlos Kong remembers these drips being "suspended in animation", basically time morphing into visual matter.

Pan Daijing's work never follows a single tempo. It is a reminder that various systems in our bodies, including the cardiovascular, metabolic, and reproductive systems have their own peripheral circadian clocks, which cycle through active and resting phases. In fact, the same is true for the trillions of cells and microbes that make us who we are. The impersonal perspective offered by her work assumes the potential liveness of everything and everyone. It expresses how everything is both present and, at the same time, latently effective.

Strengthening this sensation, time is considerably slowed down in all facets of her work. The performers' movements evoke long-exposure photographs, leaving the traces of former movements visible. It's worth noting here that, in an early interview, she refers to the dancer Noah Eshkol, who was famous for her minimalist dance choreographies and precise graphic dance notations inspired by architecture and second-order cybernetics. The treatment of individual body parts as separate instruments, of moving the human body in an "unhuman" way, reverberates in her gestural choreographies. However, her performers never dance in that way. If it were not confusing, I would say they morph like moving images.

Daijing's images, live and recorded, often seem to emerge from a void, as, for example, in the self-portrait *Metal* (2023). The artist experiments with the principles of extreme reduction, minimum contrast, and the imperceptible. She is an expert in the simple but impactful operation of subtraction. The darkness of the background and the lack of clarity in the landscape hint at the images' imaginative construction. Her images are never literal. We might interpret them as daydreams or liken them to narcotic hallucinations or to digital emanations. The first thing that comes to my mind is that they may be made for a different kind of eye.

Similarly, her landscapes usually stand in stark contrast to the norms of the conventional gallery space with its hypervigilant illumination. Daijing's attraction to threshold states, such as penumbra, gloaming, and gloom, invoke the reverse. In the dark, we don't differentiate easily. The two-channel video *Moss* (2021), which was later partly integrated into the five-channel video installation *Grief Lessons* (2023), begins with a whistling sound and the image of a lighthouse rhythmically roving over a rough sea. On the second screen, a flickering light reluctantly reveals a large and presumably empty indoor space housing an ominous apparatus. An abrupt cut suggests the clashing or colliding of times, and the image changes to a long and damp concrete tunnel. The camera looks towards the light at the end of the tunnel or to a looming apocalypse. Like the poetic streetlight, the singing tortoise, and the sweating wall, the shelter-tunnel might be a hallucinatory detail. None of the above may ever take shape (again), remaining visual echoes in the head. We create them as we meander through Pan Daijing's reality distortion fields and stare at the performers' dimly lit faces, trying to make out where they move. In *Moss* (2021), they crawl and walk over vast fields of red rubble, their bodies almost the size of small rocks.

Daijing's morphic traits reveal the obscurity of the world. Her works, in their different shapes and shades, ignite our fascination with all that remains inexplicable and out of reach. Diminishing the individual and letting the surroundings come to the fore, the impersonal perspective offered by her work is not about the end of a fractured, brittle self; rather, it constitutes a form of sublimation. Her spiritually nourishing doom is akin to awe, a mechanism for collective survival in an unstructured universe.

Dead Time Blue

Bibliography Discography

Artists' Publications
2023 Pan Daijing; Peeters, Julie; Engels, Tom. *Until Due Time, Everything Is Else*. Grazer Kunstverein, 2023.

Exhibition Catalogues
2023 Lee, Sook-Kyun, ed. *Soft and Weak Like Water*. 14 Gwangju Biennale, 2023.
2021 Basar, Shumon; Coupland, Douglas; Obrist, Hans Ulrich. *The Extreme Self*. Köln: Verlag der Buchhandlung Walther und Franz König, 2021.
Ramos, Filipa. *Flows: Bodies of Water: A Reader*. Shanghai: Power Station of Art, 2021.
2018 Bellini, Andrea; Lissoni, Andrea. *Biennale de L'Image en Mouvement 2018: The Sound of Screens Imploding*. Genève: Centre d'art Contemporain, 2018.

Articles, Essays, Interviews, Talks
2023 Kong, Carlos. "Pan Daijing, 'Until Due Time, Everything Is Else' at Grazer Kunstverein." *Mousse*, 17.11.2023.
Malašauskas, Raimundas; Januškevičiūtė, Virginija; Galinytė, Inga. "Mars Returns." *Echo Gone Wrong*, 5.1.2023.
Nahari, Ido. "Scribbles and Shakes, Notes on Pan Daijing: 'Until Due Time, Everything Is Else'." *Arts of the Working Class*, 2.11.2023.
2022 Brown, Ellie. "Awakening the Beauty of Environment: Musicality and Site-Specificity in Pan Daijing's Work." *NR Magazine* no. 15, 2022.
Cheung, Adrianna. "Experimental Chinese Artist Pan Daijing Releases 5-Part Performance-Exhibition Piece on Vinyl." *Mixmag Asia*, 4.2.2022.
Exchange, RA. "EX.593 Pan Daijing." *Resident Advisor*, 13.1.2022.
Pan Daijing. "Pan Daijing; Artist Talk." *Winter Semester 2021/22 Städelschule Lectures*. 13.1.2022.
Darenberg, Diana. "Pan Daijing:

'Echo, Moss, Spill' at Tai Kwun Contemporary." *Post-Ism*, 21.1.2022.
Tsui, Enid. "Chinese Artists' Hong Kong Installation at Tai Kwun Wrapped Music, Dance and Theatre in a Dark, Surreal Shroud to Produce Something Magical." *South China Morning Post.* 3.1.2022.
T. "Fluid Salvation in the Extreme Stillness Underneath the Mental Noise." *To Be* no. 3, 2022.
Velasco, Carolina. "Pan Daijing. Tissues." *Rockdeluxe*, 27.1.2022.
Denshinooto. デンシノオト. "Pan Daijing: Tissues." *ele-king*, 21.2.2022.

2021 Basu, Chitralekha. "On a Different Note." *China Daily, Hong Kong*, 17.12.2021.
Berezovska, Mariana. In the Mountains of Pan Daijing. *borshch Magazine*, Winter 2021.
Pan Daijing. "Composition Colloquium: Pan Daijing." *Department of Music, UC Berkeley, Composition Colloquia*. Lecture, 6.2.2021.
Geffen, Sasha. "Jade 玉观音 Pan Daijing." *Pitchfork*, 9.6.2021.
Hartmann, Andreas. " 'Jade' von Pan Daijing: Irgendwie ganz schön verstörend." *Die Tageszeitung.* 11.7.2021.
Lissoni, Andrea. "Beyond Physics. A Conversation with Pan Daijing." *Flash Art* no. 336, 2021.
Novellas, Carles. "Pan Daijing. Jade." *Rockdelux*, 22.6.2021.
Velasco, Carolina. "Pan Daijing: 'En Los Últimos Años Hemos Consumido Demasiada Música.'" *Rockdeluxe*, 13.9.2021.

2020 Ballard, Thea. "Pan Daijing." *FACT Magazine* Autumn / Winter 2020, 17.11.2020.
Fernández, Sonia in conversation with Pan Daijing *WOMXN IN MOTION,* As Part of the Symposi-

um Series *Women in the Arts and Leadership*, Hochschule für Gestaltung und Kunst Basel, Talk, October 2020.

2019 Christie, Caroline. "From Berghain to Tate Modern, Pan Daijing Heralds the Incendiary Future of Opera." *Document Journal*, October 2019.
Davis, Jared. "Thoughts Against Ambience: Sonic Tension & Void in Pan Daijing's Durational Opera 'Tissues' for the Tate Modern." *AQNB*, November 2019.

2018 Darger, H. J. "'Noise' y Experimentación: Hablamos Con La Artista China Pan Daijing." *EL PAÍS*, 26.1.2018.
Lissoni, Andrea. "Pan Daijing. Never Feeding, Only Generating." *Mousse* no. 63, 2018.
Red Bull Music Academy. "Sound Art, Composition and Experiments: Pan Daijing RBMA." Lecture, November 2018.
Burmania, Shane. "Chinese boundary-breaking artist Pan Daijing. In conversation with The Rest is Noise." *Red Light Radio*. Amsterdam: Red Light Radio at Dekmantel Festival, 8.2.2018.

2017 Ballard, Thea. "Lack. Pan Daijing, 2017." *Pitchfork*, July 2017.
Bath, Tristan. "Pan Daijing: From Powerful Techno to Dance, the Chinese Producer Takes Control." *The Wire* no. 398, April 2017.
Bondi de Antoni, Alexandra. "Das ist die Produzentin unserer liebsten Techno-Platte des Jahres. Das Debütalbum der in China geborenen Produzentin Pan Daijing lief bei uns auf Dauerschleife." *I-D Magazine* The Sounding Off Issue, no. 350, 7.12.2017.
Cornils, Kristoffer. "Pan Daijing: Groove Podcast 119." *Groove*, 11.8.2017.
Dax, Max. Pan Daijing Interview, Season 3, Episode 6. *STRRR*, 2017.

Grimm, Stephanie. "Noise-Album von Pan Daijing: Das kleine Monster in ihr muss raus." *Die Tageszeitung.* 21.8.2017.
Hartmann, Andreas. "Pan Daijings Debütalbum 'Lack': Düsenjets beim Starten zuhören." *Tagesspiegel,* October 2017.
Mitchell, Aurora. "Harsh Sonics: An Interview with Pan Daijing." *The Quietus,* March 2017.
Slater, Maya-Roisin. "Aesthetic: Pan Daijing." *Crack Magazine,* October 2017.

Discography

Pan Daijing, *Tissues*, PAN, 2022, Studio Album.
Pan Daijing, *Jade* 玉观音, PAN, 2021, Studio Album.
Pan Daijing, *Lack* 惊蛰, PAN, 2017, Studio Album.
Pan Daijing, *Sex and Disease*, Noisekölln Tapes, 2015, Cassette, Limited Edition.

EPs

Daijing & Dafeldecker, *A Page To A Corner,* iDEAL Recordings, 2018, Vinyl, 7", 45 RPM, Limited Edition.
Pan Daijing, *A Satin Sight*, Bedouin Records, 2017, Vinyl, 12", EP, Limited Edition.

Compilations

V / A, In Death's Dream Kingdom Houndstooth, 2018, 4 × Vinyl, LP, Compilation, Limited Edition
V / A, mono no aware (もののあわれ), PAN, 2017, 2 × Vinyl, LP, Compilation, Special Edition.
V / A, Vectors 3, Power Vacuum, 2017, 2 × Vinyl, LP, Compilation
V / A, Berlin Atonal Force Majeure, Berlin Atonal Recordings / Wire Magazine — Issue 40, 2017, CD, Compilation

Biographies

Emma Enderby is a curator, writer, and lecturer in modern and contemporary art. She is currently the Head of Programmes and Research / Chief Curator at Haus der Kunst München and the forthcoming Director of KW Institute for Contemporary Art, Berlin. Previously, as Chief Curator at The Shed, New York, she worked on establishing the new institution and its overall multidisciplinary programme. Her research topics include the intersection of art and ecology, technology, the reconsidering of historical (and canonical) narratives, interdisciplinary approaches, art in the public realm, and approaches to civic engagement. She has held curatorial positions in various institutions like the Public Art Fund, New York; the Serpentine Galleries, London; Whitechapel Gallery, London and Museum of Modern Art, New York. She also works as a visiting lecturer, critic, and speaker at several universities and institutions, as well as an editor and writer for multiple publications and catalogues.

Donatien Grau is a philologist, editor, scholar and museum executive. He was Head of Contemporary Programmes at Musée d'Orsay, Paris, before heading to the Musée du Louvre, where his continuing mission is to oversee the implementation of contemporary projects that echo the museum's collections. He is the author of numerous studies on literature, history and Western civilization, including *The Numismatic Memory of the Roman Empire* (Les Belles Lettres, 2022, Prix Romain de l'Académie des Floral Games) and *De Civitate Angelorum* (Yvon Lambert Editeur, 2023). He also served as a visiting professor at the National School of Visual Arts of La Cambre, Brussels. Grau's writing on art and culture has appeared in a wide range of publications. In April 2024, the inaugural edition of Alphabet Magazine will be launched under his direction as both the artistic director and editor-in-chief. Amongst his many appointments, he serves as Chair of the Association Pierre Guyotat which is dedicated to the fostering of the artist's legacy.

Mark Harwood is an artist, musician, performer, writer, event curator and publisher. He deploys a wide variety of techniques which he approaches with a sense of bypassing the cliches embedded therein to coerce a sound world that is simultaneously contemporary, foreign, beautiful, unsettling and engaging. He has collaborated with Graham Lambkin, Áine O'Dwyer, Timo van Luijk and more. His last two LP's released under his own name have become more human and personal explorations. His live performances skirt a more performative presentation of his work, often incorporate spontaneous moments of anything from comedy, pathos, or songs, as the audience is witness to an exploration of the human psyche. His writing work has included commissions by The Wire, The Quietus and Senses of Cinema, amongst others. As a publisher, he has released a large variety of recordings and books on his imprint Penultimate Press, and he co-runs the archive of Fluxus artist and composer Henning Christiansen.

Andrea Lissoni, PhD, has been the Artistic Director of Haus der Kunst München, since 2020. Formerly he was Senior Curator, International Art (Film) at Tate Modern, London, and curator at Hangar-Bicocca, Milan. At Tate he launched and co-curated new exhibition formats, such as the 2017 and 2018 live exhibition, the collection display and the live programme at the opening of the new building in 2016. He curated Philippe Parreno's Turbine Hall commission in 2016, as well as survey exhibitions of Joan Jonas and Bruce Nauman. In 2019, he co-curated the Biennale de l'Image en Mouvement *The Sound of Screens Imploding*, Centre d'Art Contemporain Genève and OGR, Turin, and participated in the international opening of CCA Tashkent, the first public contemporary art centre in Uzbekistan, where he curated the solo exhibition *Qo'rg'on Chiroq* by artist Saodat Ismailova. His programme at Haus der Kunst started in the spring of 2022 and is based on a transdisciplinary and trans-generational approach with the music residencies *Tune* connecting a series of intertwined exhibitions.

Raimundas Malašauskas is a curator and writer with a distinctively reflexive approach to writing and curating, drawing from various modes of communication. He has co-written an opera libretto (Cellar Door by Loris Greaud, Palais de Tokyo, 2008), co-produced a television show (CAC TV, Vilnius, 2004–2006), served as an agent for dOCUMENTA (13), released *Paper Exhibition*, a book of his selected writings (Sternberg Press, 2012), curated oO, Cyprus and Lithuanian Pavilions in the 55th Venice Biennale, co-curated the 9th Baltic Triennial of International Art (Vilnius, 2005), 9th Mercosul Biennial (Porto Alegre, 2013) and 9th Liverpool Biennial (2017). His most recent projects are *trust & confusion*, an eight-month-long live art exhibition at Tai Kwun Contemporary, Hong Kong (2021) and *Mars Returns*, a fourteen-hour long event at Mykolas Žilinskas Gallery, Kaunas (2022). He is currently working on his second book of selected writings, which is to be released in 2024.

Lemohang Jeremiah Mosese is a filmmaker and visual artist from Hlotse, Leriba, Lesotho. His works are a complex investigation of identity and its amorphous quality in relation to time. A self-taught filmmaker, his feature-length visual essay film *Mother, I am Suffocating, This is My Last Film About You* was selected for Final Cut in Venice, winning six awards. It premiered at the Berlinale Forum in 2019 and continues to be screened in film festivals and exhibitions, including MoMA, New York; BOZAR Brussels; Zeitz Museum of Contemporary Art Africa, Cape Town; and SAVVY Contemporary, Berlin, as a 3-channel video installation. Mosese served as an official jury member for several film festivals, including the Berlinale, Berlin; IFFR, Rotterdam; Locarno Film Festival; Eye Film-museum, Amsterdam; San Sebastian Film Festival and DOK Leipzig. He has been invited as a guest lecturer to institutions such as Cambridge University's Masters in Writing for Performance, Netherlands Film Academy Masters Program, German Film and Television Academy Berlin, and The Konrad Wolf Film University of Babelsberg.

Xue Tan is the founding Senior Curator of Tai Kwun Contemporary in Hong Kong. In the past nine years, she led the exhibition programme and worked closely with artists on over one hundred commission works. Tan's curatorial work reimagines art spaces and exhibition-making as a proactive and responsive medium for artistic experimentation. She curated Pan Daijing's solo exhibition *Echo, Moss and Spill* in 2021, the largest solo exhibition of Tino Sehgal in Asia in 2021 and recently *Maria Hassabi: I'll Be Your Mirror* in 2023. With her research focus on ecology, cosmotechnics, transnational narratives, liveness and performativity, Tan's recent curatorial projects include *Green Snake: women-centred ecologies* (2023), *trust & confusion* (2021), *Francis Alÿs, Wet feet_dry feet: borders and games* (2020), *My Body Holds Its Shape* (2020), *Phantom Plane, Cyberpunk in the Year of the Future* (2019), *Performing Society: The Violence of Gender* (2019), *Cao Fei, A Hollow in a World Too Full* (2018). Tan has led acclaimed collaborations with the Museum für Moderne Kunst in Frankfurt and the Center for Curatorial Studies of Bard College in New York.

Sarah Johanna Theurer is a curator focusing on time-based art practices and techno-social entanglements. She currently works at Haus der Kunst München where she co-curated the exhibition *Pan Daijing. Mute*, spearheaded new commissions and projects by artists including Isabelle Lewis, Carsten Nicolai, Jenna Sutela, and Wang Shui and co-curated survey exhibitions of Katalin Ladik (2023, with Hendrik Folkerts) and Fujiko Nakaya (2022, with Andrea Lissoni). She also edited the first comprehensive catalogue of Nakaya's work. Together with colleagues, she initiated the live program *Echoes* probing experiential and embodied knowledge production, as well as various projects and symposia on art and technology. Previously, she worked at the 9th Berlin Biennale and transmediale Berlin and acted as a dramaturge with performance groups including OMSK Social Club and The Agency. Theurer is the editor of this publication and publishes regularly in catalogues and magazines.

Imprint

This publication was published on the occasion of the exhibition

Pan Daijing. Mute
Haus der Kunst München
9th March 2024 — 14th April 2024

The book is published in collaboration with Tai Kwun Contemporary (TKC)

Editor   Sarah Johanna Theurer

Project Manager TKC
Daniel Szehin Ho

With contributions by
Emma Enderby
Donatien Grau
Mark Harwood
Andrea Lissoni
Raimundas Malašauskas
Lemohang Jeremiah Mosese
Xue Tan
Sarah Johanna Theurer

Proofreading   Jan Caspers
Copyediting of *Blank Spaces*
Daniel Szehin Ho (English),
Zian Chen (Mandarin Chinese)
Translations   Mary King Bradley (Mandarin Chinese to English)
Graphic Design   Lamm & Kirch, Berlin / Leipzig with Caspar Reuss
Printing / binding DZA Druckerei zu Altenburg GmbH
Image editing   Prints Professional
Typeface   Rima Grotesk
Material   Holmen TRND
Canvas Extra R

© 2024 Stiftung Haus der Kunst München, gemeinnützige Betriebsgesellschaft mbH and authors
© The artist for the reproduced works

Published by
Spector Books OHG
Harkortstraße 10
D-04107 Leipzig
www.spectorbooks.com

ISBN 978-3-95905-808-7
Printed in Germany

Stiftung Haus der Kunst München, gemeinnützige Betriebsgesellschaft mbH
Prinzregentenstraße 1
80538 München
www.hausderkunst.de

Direction
Artistic Director
Andrea Lissoni
Commercial Director
Bianca Knall
Executive Assistant /
Business Affairs Manager
Biljana Gligorić
Assistant to the Commercial Director
Iris Ludwig
Assistant to the Artistic Director
Margarita Shabaeva

Curatorial Department
Head of Programmes and Research /
Chief Curator
    Emma Enderby
Curatorial Fellow
    Lydia Antoniou
Senior Curator
    Dr. Jana Baumann
Head of Archive
    Sabine Brantl
Team Assistant
    Sylvia Clasen
Assistant to the Head of Programmes
and Research / Chief Curator
    Isabella Kredler
Curatorial Fellow
    Lydia Korndörfer
Freelance Curator, Music
    Sarah Miles
Assistant Curator
    Teresa Retzer
Curator
    Anna Schneider
Curatorial Assistant
    Radia Soukni
Curator
    Sarah Johanna Theurer
Curatorial Fellow
    Hanns Lennart Wiesner

Exhibition Coordination / Production
Head of Exhibition Coordination /
Production
    Hanna Kriegleder
Exhibition Construction
    Markus Brandenburg
Exhibition Coordination / Production
Fellow
    Katja Cox
Depot / Continuity
    Tanja Eiler
Assistant Exhibition Coord. / Production
    Leonie Kürbs
Student Assistant Exhibition Coordina-
tion / Production
    Baldwin Maslim

Communications
Head of Communication / Marketing
    Anja Fetzer

Communication Fellow
    Valentina Häberle
Video / Audio Producer
    Manuela Illera
Press and Communication
    Claudia Illi
Student Assistant Communication
    Veronika Lutz
    Juliane Wiemer
Communication Fellow
    Peggy Rudolph
Digital Communication
    Janina Vujić

Engagement, Education, Events
Head of Engagement / Participation
    Pia Linden
Education / Participation
    Camille Latreille
Visitor Service
    Thomas Ludwig
Event Management and Production
    Andrea Saul

Finance and Administration
Head of Finance and Controlling
    Thomas Kirst
Student Assistant Administration
    Andre Bagh
Assistant HR
    Jessica Fuhrmann
Accounting
    Jorge Sanchez
    Alessandro Grillo
Exhibition Supervisor
    Niels Osthorst
Procurement Manager
    Moritz Petersen
Head of HR
    Cora Szabó

Facility Management
Facility Manager
    Anton Köttl
Mail Office
    Konstantin Kamponeski
Janitor
    Roland Roppelt
    Robert Szabó

For their annual support of our programme we thank our shareholders, the Free State of Bavaria and the Gesellschaft der Freunde Haus der Kunst e. V.

We further thank our major supporter, the Alexander Tutsek-Stiftung, for their generous commitment, as well as Ulli und Uwe Kai-Stiftung.

ULLI UND UWE KAI-STIFTUNG

Tai Kwun

Head of Art
Pi Li

Art Administration Manager
Julie Lian

Curatorial Team
Curator-at-Large
Tobias Berger
Senior Curators
Ying Kwok
Xue Tan
Associate Curators
Jill Angel Chun
Louiza Ho
Shuman Wang
Assistant Curators
Claude Chan
Tiffany Leung

Exhibition Production & Technical Team
Exhibition Coordinator
Miki Hui
Senior Exhibition Manager
Pauline Kunze
Senior Registrar and Operations Manager
Jessie Mak
Assistant Registrar
Damon Lam
Art Coordinator
Kayee Cheng
Exhibition Technicians
Astria Leung
Jarvis Luk

Gallery and Docent Team
Art Education and Gallery Coordinator
Vanessa Wong
And the entire docent team

Education and Public Programmes Team
Education and Public Programmes Curator
Veronica Wong
Assistant Curator for Education and Public Programmes
Christy Chow
Education and Public Programmes Coordinators
Sonia Cheng
Gary Kwong
Christy Lee

Artists' Book Library
Associate Curator for Artists' Book Library and Public Programmes
Ingrid Pui Yee Chu

Editorial and Design
Senior Editor and Project Manager (Publications and Digital)
Daniel Szehin Ho
Chinese Editor
Grace Lai
Content and Production Coordinator
Felicity Kei Ching Wong

The Hong Kong Jockey Club

Image credits and captions

1–16 Video still, Haus der Kunst, 2024
© Pan Daijing, camera: Kleber Nascimento

41–42, 45–46
Installation view, *In Service of a Song* (2018)
Photo © Thomas Bruns.
Courtesy Galerie Isabella Bortolozzi, Berlin

39–40, 43–44
Performance view, *In Service of a Song* (2017)
Courtesy Haus der Kulturen der Welt, Berlin; Photo: Ralf Marsault / CCTV camera

53–62 Performance view, *Tissues* (2018), a performance held on the occasion of the Biennale de l'Image en Mouvement 2018. Courtesy Centre d'Art Contemporain Genève; Photo: Mathilda Olmi

63–76 Performance view, *Tissues* (2019)

85–102 Installation view, *Until Due Time, Everything is Else* (2023)
Courtesy Grazer Kunstverein; Photo: Manuel Carreon Lopez

109–118 Film still, *Avalanche* (2023)

123–134 Film still, *The Hour Between Dog and Wolf* (2024)

141–156 Solo Performance, *Untitled Series*

141, 146 Mayhem, Copenhagen
142 Private event, Paris
143 Fylkingen, Stockholm
144 Schloss Neugebäude, Vienna
145 Rockbund Museum, Shanghai
147 Queen Elisabeth Hall, London
148 Arsenic, Lausanne
149 Shanghai
150 Belgrade
151, 156 Bourse de Commerce, Paris; Courtesy of Pinault Collection; Photo: Marc Domage
152 Northcote Uniting Church, Melbourne; Courtesy of the artist and Keelan O'Hehir for Liquid Architecture
153 St John's Church, London
154 Cakeshop, Seoul
155 Villa Massimo, Rome

169, 171 Film still, *Moss* (2021)

170, 172–174, 180–181
Installation view, *Echo, Moss and Spill* (2021)
Courtesy Tai Kwun Contemporary, Hong Kong

175–179, 182–186
Performance view, *Echo, Moss and Spill* (2021)
Courtesy the artist; Camera: Dzhovani Gospodinov

195–202 Performance view, *Uncut* (2022), performance held on the occasion of Ghost 2565: Live Without Dead Time, Bangkok
Courtesy Ghost Foundation / Bangkok City City; Photo: Kanrapee Chokpaiboon

203–212 Installation and performance view, *Done Duet* (2021), commissioned by the 13th Shanghai Biennale / Power Station of Art. Courtesy of Power Station of Art, Shanghai; Photo: Chen Hao

219–232 Performance view, *Dead Time Blue* (2020)
Courtesy the artist; Camera: Dzhovani Gospodinov

245–260 Video still, Haus der Kunst, 2024, © Pan Daijing

If not otherwise indicated, Photo Courtesy the artist.